FEMALE MISSIONARIES IN INDIA

FEMALE MISSIONARIES IN INDIA

MRS. WEITBRECHT

GYAN

Published by

Gyan Publishing House
5, Ansari Road
Daryaganj, New Delhi-110002
Phone: 011-47034999, 9811692060
E-mail: books@gyanbooks.com

Distribution Network
gyanbooks.com
India, USA, Canada, UK, Australia

ISBN: 978-93-6780-211-3 (HB)

First Published, 1843

2nd Impression 2024

Printed at: Gyan Press, Delhi.

FEMALE MISSIONARIES IN INDIA
Author: MRS. WEITBRECHT

FEMALE MISSIONARIES IN INDIA.

LETTERS

FROM

A MISSIONARY'S WIFE ABROAD

TO

A FRIEND IN ENGLAND.

By Mrs. Weitbrecht.

Second Edition.

LONDON:
JAMES NISBET AND CO. BERNERS STREET.
MDCCCXLIII.

TO THE

HONOURABLE DOWAGER LADY GREY,

ONE OF THE VICE-PRESIDENTS OF THE SOCIETY FOR PROMOTING FEMALE EDUCATION IN THE EAST,

THESE LETTERS,

Which have been written with an earnest desire to aid in promoting the cause which has excited a deep and practical interest in her Ladyship's best sympathies, are, by her permission, respectfully dedicated,

By her obedient

And obliged Servant,

THE AUTHOR.

PREFACE.

I HAVE been requested by the nearest connection of the writer of these Letters to append a short preface to them. To this request I have acceded, and I trust that my desire to oblige a friend, whom I have known ever since he studied in Basle, in the year 1826, may be my excuse for this undertaking. Any recommendation of this work will, I apprehend, be considered useless, when it is known under what circumstances it has been written. It is the result of the observation of one who has herself seen all that she describes, and who is enabled to trace, in her own experience, the good or ill consequences which have followed her designs. Rules derived from actual experience must, in cases of missionary enterprise, be especially important. Moreover, in the case of the writer of these observations, her notions have not been formed from short examination, or in a life of little or of trifling occupation, but by passing through almost every situation into which such a labourer was enabled, in her circumstances, to enter.

One point will be demonstrated in this work, the importance of *female agency* in the work of missions. The labours of females in the extension of the kingdom of Christ is subject of divine record. "Priscilla," the wife of Aquilla, was the apostle's fellow "helper in Jesus Christ," and "Tryphena and Tryphosa" laboured in the Lord. Moreover, from the time when the sufferings of our Lord called forth the sympathy of the women who were about him, to this time, when females have been led to engage in the work of missions, we have seen the affectionate heart of the sex successfully occupied in communicating that sympathy which it has been peculiarly in their power to afford. And in our own days many individuals may be found who have attained to the knowledge of divine things, through the persevering kindness and instruction of such teachers as these. Attached to various missionary institutions, many females have laboured singly, especially amidst the young; and in connection with others, how often have we seen such labourers engaged in assisting to alleviate trial and to dispense help; how many husbands have found in their partners the wise counsellor, the encouraging fellow-helper, the calmer of his troubled spirit, the messenger of comfort, directing him to God, and assisting him in drawing down his blessing. Women, as missionaries, have afforded the most important examples of the happiness of domestic life, when regulated on christian principles. What instruction have they given to the heathen, of the extreme folly of degrading females, as they are accustomed to do; and on the other hand, how often have they exhibited to the degraded partners of a brutal husband, the blessing of religious principle, in making them happy, useful, and independent.

But in order to take every advantage of her position, a female missionary must possess the knowledge and the virtues which will make her shine brightly amongst those with whom she is placed. She must have her understanding well instructed in divine things. She must be spiritually established in those doctrinal truths, which can alone lead her to true faith and holy obedience. She must have her heart purified by faith, and her conversation regulated by the highest standard of practical godliness. Moreover, in order to assist others, she must be well instructed in a variety of points, in those especially in which she may meet the enquiries of the higher order of native heathen amongst whom she may be placed, and in which she may direct others in the lower walks of life. So that, to whatever state of life she is called, as a woman, a wife, a mother, a teacher, a friend, a mistress, she may be a consistent and faithful model and teacher.

To instruction in all these points, this little work will lead an enquirer. It is designed to teach a female, who is desirous of entering on missionary work, the means of effecting the greatest measure of good, and to encourage such an individual in going forward to attain the blessedness attendant upon the performance of this service. Would that the end of this little publication might be, to lead some who may read it to enter upon that course, which the writer of these letters has so happily followed, to seek a field of labour amongst the hundreds of millions of degraded females, whose condition cries out for help, to engage herself in a duty of the highest honour, that of a labourer in Christ's service, and so to labour that she may receive the best reward, the crown, which is especially the missionary's portion, at the last day.

FRANCIS CUNNINGHAM.

Lowestoft Vicarage,
May 6th, 1843.

FEMALE MISSIONARIES IN INDIA.

LETTER I.

INTRODUCTORY.

My dear Friend,

You have often requested me to give you in a few letters the results of my experience in the female department of missionary labours in India, both as it respects the class of characters best fitted for engaging in it, and explanatory of the peculiar nature of the work. I have been prevented from making an effort to meet your wishes hitherto only by want of leisure; but I have just at present some time which I can devote to the subject, and as the delay has added to my experience, which now extends to upwards of ten years, I feel better prepared to undertake a delineation of the subject, whch is truly one of deep moment, and one which has hitherto received, apparently, too little consideration.

All I can attempt is, to express to you in a plain and simple manner the convictions of my own mind. To do justice to such a subject is beyond my power; but perhaps the information I may impart, and the suggestions I may be able to offer, may lead some better qualified persons to take up the pen in its service, and under the divine blessing, even my humble and imperfect attempt may be productive of benefit, and aid in its small measure that high and holy cause, which must be so dear to the heart of every true missionary—the cause of Christ in a heathen land!

I will aim to avoid unnecessary repetitions, though the near connection of some of the points on which I must speak, and which it yet seems necessary, for the sake of clearness and simplicity, to treat of in different letters, will make it difficult for me to do so entirely. I wish to be concise, but I must be explicit, because I am writing chiefly for those who are either entirely ignorant, or very imperfectly informed, on a subject which has, from being familiarized to my own mind by a long contemplation of it, and by so many years actual practical trial of it, lost to me its freshness, though not its importance. The sentiments I wish to diffuse, may be as new to the generality of those who may read my letters, as they are old and established in my own mind.

My first letter, succeeding this introductory one, will have reference to the disposition of mind with which we should enter upon missionary work, with some indirect references to the duty and privilege of engaging in it personally, and to the encouragements contained in the Word of God to those who practically leave all and follow Him. In the second I will try to describe the characters fitted for engaging in this work, without reference to the individual being married or unmarried. There is, I know, a diversity of opinion on the point of single ladies going out to India, to engage in mission work; but as in practice they do it, and as there are societies both in England and on the continent which are organized for preparing and sending them forth, it seems desirable to describe the character and qualities that should appertain to the female labourer, irrespective of her being married or otherwise.

I will follow this by a letter more particularly descriptive of the domestic character of a missionary's wife, where many points have to be noticed that the general nature of the former letter would render it irrelevant to bring forward there.

In the next I will say something on the preparation necessary for engaging in missionary work, and in the succeeding one will allude, a little in detail, to the peculiar difficulties connected with it, though it will scarcely be possible to avoid frequent reference to these in all the letters, so that this part of my subject must be in a degree anticipated. It seems, however, desirable to give a connected view of them notwithstanding.

A letter on the kind of efforts that may most profitably be made, as calculated to promise success, and a short one in conclusion, introducing a few remarks upon the engagement of single ladies, which strike me as of importance to be noticed, will, I think, contain all I can profitably bring before your notice. I may perhaps, occasionally relate an anecdote to elucidate my meaning, and I shall be careful to confine myself in all I advance with regard to plans and efforts, to those I can speak of with confidence from my own experience, merely noticing others in a more general way.

I almost fear that the headings of my letters may not be considered as perfectly definite, because encouragements, cautions, and casual remarks must occasionally be introduced, where the subject being treated of seems to require them, and where they can be brought home with more effect than in their regular place.

I am not writing for logicians, but for simple-minded Christians; and all my desire is, to say something that these may find useful and practical. I have, however, tried to the best of my ability to make the headings as appropriate to the subjects treated of under them as I can, and I hope you may consider them so.

I think I may say, that if a deep sense of the importance of the subject, and of my own personal deficiencies and short-comings as a missionary's wife, can teach me how to write, I shall not fail to pourtray it correctly and vividly, but above all, I desire to be taught of Him who alone giveth true wisdom.

I hope it will be understood by all who may read these letters, that they are offered chiefly in the way of suggestion and advice. I would by no means be supposed to affirm, that all the qualities alluded to are indispensable, or that the entire character drawn out, is the only one which can in its perfect form be useful, but great things should certainly be aimed at, and our model and standard should be high, as it is far easier and more natural to us to descend, than to ascend, and to go below, rather than above the mark.

In this introductory letter I will take the precaution of remarking, that when reading any thing about India in Europe, it is necessary to bear in mind, that the remarks of the writer, as far as they relate to climate and customs, can only be considered to apply immediately and with perfect correctness, to that particular part of the country in which the writer usually resides. India is only a name given by us to an immense extent of country, quite as large as the whole of Europe, exclusive of Russia. It is peopled by those who differ much from each other in language, habits, &c.; and what applies to one province, as for instance, to Bengal, does not apply with equal force, and sometimes not at all, to other and distant parts. The people and their religion are one to a certain extent, but not I should think, in a greater degree than the different nations of Europe professing the reformed faith are one. The chief part of my experience has been in Bengal, and it is only with respect to that part of India that my remarks must be considered entirely to apply. The little that I have seen of other parts has only shewn me, how great the dissimilarity in many respects between the north, and south, and east, and west, the inhabitants of the coast, and those inland. What one may do without detriment to the health in one place, I have proved to be very injurious in another, so that our only safety is in taking the advice of those accustomed to the particular province to which we may go. I would have this borne in mind, when reading the rules I have appended to my last letter.

I have now only to beg the union of your fervent prayers with mine, my dear friend, that the glory of God may be promoted by this feeble attempt, and to subscribe myself

Yours affectionately,

M. Weitbrecht.

LETTER II.

ON THE DISPOSITION OF MIND WITH WHICH WE SHOULD ENTER UPON MISSIONARY WORK.

My dear Friend,

It is not exactly in my plan to say much on the duty and privilege of engaging in missionary work, in the way of exciting, persuading, and urging females to enter upon it, nor is it necessary. There are many masterly works extant, in which this subject is treated at large, and powerfully proved, and to these most can gain access. It is true that in them, no particular reference may be made to female duty; but I believe it is now generally allowed, that female influence and co-operation is necessary, in a greater or less degree, in evangelizing the world; and the arguments, which apply to the church as a body, are intended for both sexes. I would, therefore, rather recommend the perusal and study of the books which bring this important subject before the mind in all its force and bearings, than attempt to advance what I am not able to say half so well as others have said it, and to suggest self-examination on the question, of whether or not *we*, as individuals, have any ground to suppose ourselves called to engage in missionary labours.

There is a great diversity of opinion, even among experienced Christians and missionaries, as to the propriety and necessity of *single* females engaging in mission work. It is certainly a very difficult and delicate subject to speak upon, and one which requires to be treated with great prudence and caution.

Our sex is naturally so much under the influence of feeling, that we are particularly liable to be led astray by it, and to form wrong conclusions, guided by impulse rather than principle. A double degree of care is therefore necessary in referring to female duty in this respect; and those whose minds are at all led to think of engaging in mission work, have great need to be very jealous over themselves, and very slow in deciding on offering themselves for it.

They must first feel fully satisfied that there is no duty demanding their prior attention at home, such as the care and support of aged parents, or other near relatives; that outward circumstances are favourable, and that health and constitution are good; that such friends as are capable of forming a correct judgment approve of their desire; and that previous education and discipline, have in some degree, prepared them for it, while no impediments offer, the overcoming of which will, in any degree, involve the consistency of the christian character, or any thing beyond *personal* sacrifice. A due measure of consideration to these preliminary points may save much future perplexity, and enable them to avoid the danger of running before they are sent.

These points being fairly settled, they will be at liberty to take up the subject, to meditate upon it, pray over it, seek the best and most prudent advice respecting it, and be fully persuaded in their own minds that they are really in some good degree suited for it, and called to it, before they venture to think of taking any decided steps regarding future engagement in it. It is not the warm and lively sympathies for the poor heathen produced by hearing an animated discourse upon missions, or by listening to the thrilling appeals made at a missionary meeting, that will induce the right state of mind for judging ourselves. These means *may* first arouse us to a feeling of the claims of the heathen, and to a consciousness of our own responsibility to them, as those who possess the knowledge of that "everlasting Gospel" which is to be proclaimed to every creature under heaven; but it must be in the retirement of the closet, in our cool and quiet hours, when our souls are alone with God, that we can properly judge and examine ourselves in this matter. From the tenor of the succeeding letters, I hope it will be quite evident that nothing but very deep and strong principles can enable any one to become an efficient or really valuable missionary labourer, and none should venture to enter upon the field, but those who have reason to believe they possess such principles.

Perhaps some may here say it is impossible

for us to be faithful judges in our own case, but this is not so difficult as it may at first sight appear. We generally know pretty well, or can ascertain what our friends think of us; and, by comparing their opinions with our own inward experience, and the workings and impulses of our own minds; and aiding ourselves by again comparing the *results* of our inward principles, as exhibited in our practice, we may come to a pretty correct conclusion regarding ourselves. Of course, I take it for granted, in speaking of friends, that they are judicious and faithful friends, and not fond and partial ones; and I would also add, that we must judge our future selves by our present selves, so to speak; for what we are in our present sphere, the same shall we be in our future sphere. We must not imagine that when surrounded by the sights and practices of heathenism, we shall be excited to zeal, and energy, and devotedness, if we are not zealous, and energetic, and devoted where we are. The very contrary will be our experience, as many who have engaged in missionary work on mistaken grounds can well attest. There is no better and safer criterion for us to judge ourselves by, than our present actual experience, engagements, and tastes. If we are habitually prayerful, humble, and self-denying in Europe, so shall we be in India, or wherever called, in the providence of God to labour, the grace of God continuing to aid us, and *vice versâ*. We must not attempt to delude ourselves with the idea, that to labour among the poor degraded heathen, is a delightful and heart-cheering employment, for as far as nature is concerned it is precisely the opposite. One cannot too strongly depict the difficulties and trials of missionary work, and I believe they must be felt to be understood rightly. In the female department especially, we must be content, and must be willing, to be "hewers of wood and drawers of water," and be very thankful to have an opportunity of being so engaged. It is quite true, that missionary work *is* both heart-cheering and delightful, as viewed in connection with the promises of God, and with the recompence of the reward; and in the contemplation of these, we may indeed call ourselves happy and privileged labourers; but it is, nevertheless, a work involving extreme self-denial, as all who faithfully labour in it well know. I do not mean by this, that the missionary in India has any very extraordinary temporal privations to bear. On the contrary, we have many alleviations to the heat, suitable food, very tolerable servants, generally speaking pretty good dwellings, and I may say, all we can reasonably desire for the comfort of our bodies, as far as one can speak of comfort in what is to us such an unnatural climate: but our mental trials, and our spiritual privations, are great, and of no ordinary kind; we feel the debilitating influence of the moral climate of India on our souls, *more* than we feel that of its natural climate on our bodies, and it needs more spiritual strength to bear up against the former, than bodily strength to sustain the latter. Hence the necessity of those well-grounded motives for entering upon the work, to which reference has been made. "We want," says a devoted missionary, "*principle*, deep, generous, glowing, mighty principle: a sufficient impulse to all exertion and sacrifice: the fruit in the soul of all the glorious motives of the cross."

From the tenor of the preceding remarks it will be conjectured, that I am not averse to the idea of single ladies engaging in missionary work, but as in this I wish my views to be clearly apparent, I will now proceed to make a few direct remarks upon this point.

It strikes me that some consideration should be allowed to women as well as to men in this respect, and that when an individual has a strong desire, and earnest longing to enter upon labours in a heathen land, and manifests a decided suitability for such labours, no discouragements should be offered simply on the ground of sex, as such persons certainly give promise of being likely to prove more zealous and efficient than others, who have never been led to desire similar dedication. The state of society in our days makes the subject one of difficulty, but I believe that with regard to the question, as to why christian women, whom God has prepared for missionary usefulness, should not emulate those women who laboured in the Gospel in apostolic times, there can scarcely be a diversity of opinion; for surely *women*, either single or married, are as indispensable to the successful operations of missions, as to the progress and well-being of society in christian lands. And since married women are not always able to command sufficient leisure, for all the calls that are made on them, single ones may well step in to fill the posts, which seem more particularly their sphere and calling, that of school teachers, superintendents, and so on. We read in the earlier history of the church very striking instances of female devotedness and usefulness. Some women are mentioned by name, as having crossed the sea to convert heathen females, and as labouring for many years with much success; and I believe it will be allowed, that if female education has received an impulse in Bengal, it has been chiefly through the efforts of those who came out single, which is the best argument in favour of the plan, and the one least likely to be gainsaid. Mr. Smith, of Madras, writes, "unmarried females of sound constitution, superior qualifications, and eminent piety, should be encouraged to enter the mission field." I have often heard testimonies equally strong.

But though I have said so much on this particular, I must remark that I do not wonder at the opinions entertained by many missionaries and others, respecting the unadvisedness of bringing or sending out single ladies to India to engage in mission work, and I will briefly refer to my reasons.

There have been among those excellent women who have devoted themselves to the heathen, some who have nobly redeemed the pledge they gave to the church, and whose example and perseverance has spoken powerfully in favour of the plan of engaging and sending forth single females. It is unnecessary to mention names, and sufficient to refer to facts. Such individuals came out actuated by the right and true missionary spirit, and have shewn what it is possible for single females to accomplish.

Had all acted thus, there would doubtless have been few objectors to the engagement of single females in the work of missions, but when those who come to a heathen country, professing to be willing to endure self-denial to its utmost extent, shrink from it on its first approach, and readily resign those labours to which they had in name devoted their lives, at the first temptation that assails them, people are immediately disposed to become dissatisfied with the system, and to lay the blame on it. Forgetting,—or perhaps not fully knowing, the various instances of excellent and exemplary women who have been faithful to their professions, they condemn the whole, on account of the inconsistencies of the few, though all who are acquainted with the history of missions should be aware, that failures in each department, ever have, and ever will occasionally occur, both with men and women.

In a country like India, where there is not exactly the same high standard of public opinion as in England, where *motives* are canvassed, and individuals judged in their actions in a way that can scarcely be described, and much less conceived, by those who have no idea of the state of society as it exists abroad, it is doubly necessary to be on one's guard, for too much goes by prejudice and a sort of false sympathy, that is very injurious, and more mistaken impressions seem to result from one or two failures, where every thing is known and talked of, than right impressions, from numerous proofs of success, which make no particular noise. Thus missionaries are blamed, and keenly feeling the ground that is given for reproach, they come to the conclusion, that it is better not to make the attempt than to run the risk of such painful occurrences.

I am happy to say, that out of a considerable number of ladies whom I have known as coming out single to engage in missionary work, I remember scarcely one instance where they have not in a greater or less degree been faithful to the spirit of their profession, though some perhaps may consider, not perhaps exactly to the letter of it. I however think that extreme discretion should be observed by all parties engaged in preparing and sending out female labourers, and I shall take occasion to refer again to this hereafter.

In the meanwhile I would repeat, that those who would engage in this warfare *must* first count the cost, for trials, and severe ones, they must be prepared to endure *without* shrinking, and if they are not prepared for these, it is far better that they remain at home.

The preceding remarks run more in the style of caution than of encouragement, because I feel so deeply, from what I have seen and known in India, how important it is that all who engage in mission work, should be fully informed of the arduous nature of it, and be made to understand clearly the kind of life they must expect to encounter, as far as it is possible for descriptions and representations to make it apparent. Far be it from me, however, to discourage any whose "hearts God has touched," for I have to acknowledge, with gratitude, the valuable aid I have derived from my fellow-helpers during a period of several years—aid which I had tried in vain to obtain in India; and though I believe that in large towns, such as Calcutta or near it, it is not so difficult as I found it in the country to obtain East Indian assistants; and it is perhaps, becoming easier every year, yet I cannot doubt that single ladies of the right sort, may still be very useful, when received by mutual consent into missionary, or other devoted families, who need and apply for them, and are willing and anxious to avail themselves of their help, though I would decidedly say, *only* to *such;* for it must ever be remembered that a *young woman* is, of all creatures in the world, the *least* calculated and the least intended to stand *alone*, and that particularly in a country like India. These points should, of course, be satisfactorily settled previously, and no time will eventually be lost by all parties concerned determining to have the clearest understanding, and the most definite arrangements possible made, but this will more properly come under consideration hereafter.

I will not close this letter without adding a few words of direct encouragement, though, as I observed at the commencement, very little necessity exists for me to enlarge on these points, and it scarcely comes within my plan or object, which is more to advise and direct individuals, who have been already awakened to the claims of the heathen on their sympathy and aid.

I am writing to those who "know the

grace of our Lord Jesus Christ;" who know *his* compassion for souls, his love for *us*, and that nothing can please or honour Him more, than self-devotedness to his cause among the heathen; who fully understand that he who lives to himself is not a Christian, and feel that every part and property of our nature, and every moment of our existence, having been bought and paid for with the precious blood of Christ, is not our own, but charged with a duty to Him who thus redeemed it. All our powers being held by us, as a precious trust for Christ, must be employed for Him in the way that seems most likely to prove effectual. His cross supplies us with a motive sufficiently strong to impel us forward, and it is not left for us to choose or not, but his Word declares, that Him we are *bound* to glorify with our bodies and spirits, which are his, and not our own. His mission from heaven to Calvary contains in it the spring and principle of all other missions, and there is not a moment in which the command is suspended, "Be not weary in well doing," while every believing act of good will add a ray to the radiance of that crown, which we hope hereafter to cast at our Saviour's feet.

Christ died for the good of man, and He expects that all who call themselves His followers, should live for the same blessed object which prompted Him to be "stricken, smitten of God, and afflicted." *We*, as individuals, are brought under obligations to Christ, that we may be engaged and engrossed for the salvation of our fellow immortals, and He who requires this of us supplies us with power, by imparting to us the promised help of his Holy Spirit, who bestows on us an abundance of heavenly influence to fit us for our duty: He even allures us to cultivate the tree, by promising us that we shall reap the fruit, and we may be sure that, in due season, we shall reap, if we faint not.*

* Just before writing the above remarks, I was privileged to read a most beautiful Essay on Christian Missions lately published, by the perusal of which my mind was so deeply impressed, that I believe I have embodied several of the ideas therein presented in these two pages. I cannot answer for the actual expressions, and therefore I have not ventured to mark a single sentence; but I feel convinced that I am indebted to that Essay for several of the senti-

Arduous and trying as missionary work is, I do believe and can affirm from experience, that it is the most happy and blessed work, the most high and holy calling, in which the Christian can be privileged to engage, when faith is strong and lively, and when it is viewed, as it ever should be, through . that medium. As it has its own peculiar sorrows, so it has its joys, with which a stranger to it intermeddleth not. An indifferent and careless labourer may be an unhappy, cheerless labourer, but a spiritual, prayerful, devoted woman must, though surrounded by much calulated to grieve, depress, discourage, and overwhelm her, be a Christian of no ordinary experience and elevation of mind, and be unwilling to exchange positions with those who are apparently, the most favoured members of the christian church; and if we "prove God," *i.e.* take Him at his word, He will bless us so largely, that all needful grace will be bestowed.*

ments I have expressed, for it so entirely embodied my own previous ideas, that every word seemed to fasten itself on my memory.

* On one occasion, when a lady, who was the wife

Although therefore, I am anxious to caution, and even to discourage those who do not look upon mission work from the highest

of a civilian, was stopping over a Sabbath in the mission house, the delicate state of her health prevented her from attending the English service in the evening, and she remained at home with me. At the usual hour the native christian women assembled in a large room in the mission house, and took their customary places on a mat on the floor, forming a circle around the lights, which were placed in the centre of the room. A very pious native Christian, who had a great gift in expounding Scripture, but who was quite blind, and unable to read, sat at the top of the room, and the orphan girls in front within the circle of the women.

The lady referred to sat in a recess which commanded a view of the whole scene. The service was commenced by the catechist giving out a Bengalee hymn from memory, and setting the tune, which was also native music. Every individual joined, and when the singing ceased, the whole company prostrated themselves according to the oriental method, and a short and fervent prayer was offered. The exposition was very simple, but just suited to the capacities of the hearers, who were evidently deeply interested. After the concluding singing and prayer, the women and girls rose, and with smiling faces passed in rotation before the lady and myself, and point of view, and who are not quite persuaded of being fully prepared for its trials, self-denials, and disappointments, and who would enter upon it with far too sanguine anticipations of its outward and present enjoyments; you will easily perceive how I, in truth, and from my most powerful inward convictions, in real fact, regard it, and how much satisfaction I should have, in welcoming one after another, of really suitable and devoted labourers, to India's shores to engage in it. I long to see our numbers enlarged, by an accession of right-minded individuals, but I do believe that only these can be of any avail, and that we are better without inadequate helpers.

What I have said in this letter, though written more particularly with reference to single females, will I hope, be equally useful for the consideration of those who contemplate a union with missionaries, and I have had

made their salaam on leaving. The lady was quite overcome, and exclaimed with the deepest feelings, "Oh, this is true happiness; this is delightful; a missionary's wife must be, indeed, a happy woman!"

them equally in view while writing; their christian character and attainments need to be of the highest possible order, as I shall more particularly endeavour to depict in a future letter.

Yours, &c.

M. W.

LETTER III.

ON THE CHARACTERS FITTED FOR ENGAGING IN MISSIONARY WORK.

My dear Friend,

IN the preceding letter I have prepared you to expect that I take a very high view of the class of females who should engage in mission work, and I believe that too high a standard can scarcely be raised. It is no common engagement they enter upon, and it requires no common character rightly and consistently to fulfil it. I would, as I have before said, discourage none "whose hearts God has touched," but as in the case of men, so I am convinced in that of women likewise, it requires superior persons in every respect, both by nature and grace. Such as are weak in faith, or whose minds are easily affected, are quite unfit, while those of strong, healthy, cheerful piety, founded on clear scriptural principles, will wear well, and work on through all difficulties.

I must first refer to the physical qualities which should be possessed, and will begin with age and constitution. From all I have seen, I am inclined to the opinion which seems most natural, and which is I believe generally held, that the younger an individual enter upon labours in a climate so essentially different to her native one, the better as a rule, though this of course, admits of exceptions, and I have known of several exceptions, which were not failures. It is quite necessary that maturity of mind and character be possessed, and when these are displayed, the earlier an individual venture on an exchange of climate, the more likely will her constitution be to assimilate well with it. The mind and habits are also more flexible at an earlier age, and can more readily form themselves to the altered circumstances in which they will be placed, and above all it may be said, that humanly speaking, a longer term of usefulness is likely to be enjoyed by the individual who engages in the work.

As it regards the constitution and general health, both should of course be good. It may not be necessary or perhaps desirable, that one be particularly hale or strong, but a healthful constitution, without a predisposition to any particular disease or weakness, is most desirable. All those of inflammatory habits, and such as have a tendency of blood to the head, should be very cautious in venturing on a tropical climate. Persons of cool and even temperament, slow pulse, tranquil minds, and a good degree of nerve, would seem the best suited for it, for it may be observed, that a hot climate has an immense influence upon the nervous system. I purpose adding a few rules relative to health, in an appendix, interspersed with such remarks as may elucidate them.

I have heard it remarked, that it is impossible for what is commonly called a passionate or bad tempered person, to enjoy good health in India, and though this may not be strictly correct, there is certainly some ground for the assertion. I look upon a sweet even temperament as of the first importance, particularly as it relates to females, who have from the nature of their engagements, more to try the temper than the other sex. An Indian climate, and native servants and habits, tell upon the best temper, and one requires to be extremely watchful over oneself in this particular. I have known the most lamentable effects to arise from yielding to the temptation of giving way to temper, even among missionary females, which induces me to lay great stress upon it; and I ought to add, that it is important not only as it affects ourselves, but in its influence upon the natives, who always appreciate it very highly, while they are disposed to make little allowance for the want of it. Nothing but deep piety, and living near to God can enable us, in many cases, to preserve the equanimity of what may be called our natural temper, under all the provocations to which it is liable; but it is so intimately connected with both health and usefulness, that it becomes one of our first duties to guard it in every possible way, and by every direct and indirect effort. Activity and energy, both of mind and body, must be combined with this habitual equanimity, and these together, will induce that cheerfulness of spirit in the performance of our daily duties, which will prove, not only one of the best preservatives of our health, but one of the chief auxiliaries to our usefulness. With a quiet temper, we may be passively useful only, and with an energetic spirit actively useful only, but the union of both is necessary; and both should be aimed at, and prayed for. A tropical climate has not less influence upon our energies, than it has upon our tempers, and there are few indeed who do not in some degree suffer loss in this respect. With regard to all our abilities, we must remember that we are upon enemies' ground, and that we shall feel continual need of the Saviour's injunction, to "Watch and pray, lest we enter into temptation, for though the spirit may be willing, the flesh is weak." It is often a great effort truly, to maintain bodily activity at the most trying seasons of the year, when the heat is fearfully oppressive: but those who do so, are well repaid for it in every way, and do not in reality suffer so much either in strength or spirits, as those who yield to languid indolence. It must ever be borne in mind,—so intimately is our physical and intellectual nature connected, that activity of mind is most likely to produce activity of body, and I must therefore guard what I have said on this particular by one cautionary remark, *i. e.* that when the state of the health, or other causes, make quietness and suspension from our usual duties desirable, we should patiently acquiesce, and willingly resign ourselves to a season of rest. There is much true wisdom and prudence in this, for an active mind is distinct from a restless unquiet mind, and it is a duty to make the best of our strength by duly husbanding it ;—to bend the bow too forcibly is as great an error as to relax it unduly.

I may next say a few words on general habits and manners. The habits should be neat, orderly, diligent—we do very much by our habits—if they are good we can get through a much larger amount of work, with less effort to ourselves, than if they are the contrary. I was never tired of admiring a dear missionary sister, (now with God,) who particularly excelled in this respect, and who thereby gave a grace and a finish to every thing she attempted, which made her schools, and all her arrangements, additionally interesting to those who saw them. I am persuaded that we very much need attention to these points, in our orphan and boarding schools, for we have quite to form the natives in these respects, and as outward order has so much to do with inward order, which again is very essential to due mental progress and improvement, a good degree of care should be directed towards our habits. Order may be said to be among one of the "trifles, that form the *sum* of human things," if that can properly be called a trifle, which involves in it such important consequences, as does the observation of orderly habits.

Our manners should also receive attention, for manner, as has been observed, is *something* with all, and *every thing* with some. Piety and courtesy are not averse to each other, but coalesce well together, and pleasing affable behaviour has its effect, when it springs from right and sincere principle; and it ought to be cultivated, because it is some check upon natural selfishness, as well as because it commands respect and attention. I have seen very excellent women, who thought it hard and unreasonable, to be expected to be polite and courteous, and I have heard it remarked by others, as the chief fault to be regretted in such individuals. It seems to me that in India especially, it is very desirable to pay a degree of attention to manner, that might hardly be necessary elsewhere. It is much thought of by European society, and though it is a thing of inferior moment in itself, it is not without its use, and its influence in recommending our work. Besides this, we naturally love among ourselves, those of an affectionate, conciliating deportment, whose address is amiable and engaging, and on no people does a gentle, affable, and yet dignified manner, produce a greater effect than on the Hindus.

I come now to speak of education, which should be good and solid, for that which is superficial and showy we have no need, and accomplishments are neither necessary or essential, but a well read, well informed mind, and an ability to express oneself with ease and facility in writing, are very important.

To have learned a foreign language *well*, and *thoroughly*, will be a help, not because we need the use of any other European language than English in India, but because the study and mental industry, necessary for the acquisition of a language, has so good an effect in disciplining and schooling the mind, that it will then be much easier to sit down to the native language, and to persevere in gaining a good knowledge of it, which is of the first importance. A thorough acquaintance with geography and history is very desirable, and to be a good arithmetician is desirable likewise. All kinds of useful knowledge, (and I know of none that may not be called useful, and be turned to a good and practical account in India,) will be found valuable, but chiefly a certain cleverness, as it is usually called, or a dexterity and aptness, in doing every thing which falls within the ordinary sphere of female duty, especially the cleverness of the hand, which so adds to a capability for general usefulness. The arts of sewing, knitting, rug-work, embroidery, and others, are of more value than many may be inclined to think. The present stage of progress, with regard to female education in India, is a very humble one, and we cannot force intellect forward all at once; every improvement on that state of degradation, in which the women of India have been for ages, will progress slowly and gradually, and none must be disappointed upon entering on their work among them to find, as many have been, that a part of their valuable time is to be spent in teaching handiworks, instead of being wholly occupied in imparting intellectual knowledge. And not only must we allow for the low state of the female mind, but the class of children of whom our schools are composed must be considered. These are mostly of the humbler orders, both actually and in ability, and do not therefore need to be trained as literary characters, even were it possible to make them such, but into good, sensible, industrious wives and mothers. The majority of them require at present, no greater degree of literary knowledge, than to read well in their own language, and no greater enlargement of mind, than to understand what they read, so as to bring it into practical use. Diligent habits are of the utmost importance, and if we succeed in training them to these, we may rejoice, for a host of evils which result from their natural and heathenish apathy, are thereby corrected, and that more effectually than they could be, by making them scholars, while such habits will have the best influence on their *religious*, as well as moral character. The disappointment to which I have alluded is no matter of wonder, considering the erroneous views which too much prevail in England, regarding our converts, schools, &c.; but it shews the necessity that exists for endeavouring to give correct ideas on these points. I had no idea when I first arrived in India of the desirableness of many things, that appeared quite evident when fairly brought to view. The climate does not admit of that out-of-doors activity, which occupies so much of our time at home, and constant mental employment is too fatiguing, both for us and our pupils, during the heat of the day. The domestic business of orphan and boarding schools devolves chiefly on the elder girls, and is undertaken by them in turns, so that a large portion of time remains to be filled up with some sitting occupation. The few children in a school of thirty or forty, who may be found possessing a larger share of ability, and to be capable of more application than the rest, and to whom it is desirable to give a more extended education, fall under the same remark, for they too need relaxation from mental effort, and cannot obtain it better than by joining the others in their sewing and knitting.

The very knowledge of these things, for their own sake, is valuable to these poor females, for it makes them more useful, both to their families, and to society at large; and when it is remembered in addition, that the women in Bengal, in their heathen state, spend all their time which is not occupied in domestic duties, in absolute idleness, unless they are very poor and must work out of doors or take service, it will clearly appear how we have to fight against their desultory habits, in every shape. I have found by experience that they do by degrees acquire a taste for, and a degree of satisfaction in quiet useful employments, which gives a sort of zest to their lives, and disposes them to more diligence in mental ones. I have observed too, that the native christian women, who have been converted after marriage, though seldom able, especially when they have families, to learn to read, can generally be taught to sew or knit, and thereby to improve in industry, and as a consequence to become raised in their general character.

A female engaged in missionary labour should further be distinguished by good sense, as well as by that truly valuable quality common sense, which I may remark by the way is so necessary, that without it, all other sense is comparatively valueless. Good sense teaches one to act with propriety and consistency under all circumstances. It shews us our proper position, in every sphere in which we may be placed, and enables us to distingush the niceties of the relation we sustain to others. It fits us to be an ornament to the circle in which we move, and to fulfil all our engagements in a judicious way. It is therefore almost indispensable to our character as missionary females, called to stand out, as it were, and maintain an eminence before the world.

I have before remarked, that accomplishments are not essential, though as education advances in our orphan and boarding schools they may become valuable. A knowledge of singing is however very desirable, as Hindu children take great delight in it, and seem to have the ability to excel in it, and I would always recommend a person to acquire it, so as to be able to sing in concert, and to teach the children to do the same, as is universally the practice in all the humbler schools in Germany. It is both interesting to others, and delightful to oneself, to be able to enjoy this recreation, and it greatly heightens the pleasure of young and old in the public services of God, to join in the singing, while it has otherwise a happy effect upon native children in various ways.

I must not omit to notice very pointedly here, what I have slightly hinted at before, that a certain degree of aptitude for languages is most desirable, for all oriental tongues are in their construction, vocabulary, and entire train of ideas, so completely different to western languages, that they may all be termed, for females particularly, more or less difficult. Perseverance may and will do a great deal, but without some degree of aptitude, it can scarcely be expected to accomplish every thing.

Hitherto there have been few females comparatively, who have acquired more than a slight and imperfect acquaintance with the native languages; but this is very much to be lamented, and though it is no matter of surprise, considering the trials and disadvantages against which they have had to struggle, yet it is a point on which we should aim to improve in future. Many may be disposed to think, that a person can be very useful with but little knowledge of the language, if she have tact and ability in other respects; and so she may, but it cannot be doubted, that it would greatly increase her sphere of usefulness, to be able to express herself fully and intelligibly on any subject she wishes to bring forward. I do not mean that we need have such a knowlege of the language as is necessary for missionaries, who have to preach and dispute in it; but we certainly should have so much as to enable us to address the school children and native christian women in a plain and familiar way, and to pray with them, persuade them, exhort and direct them. We shall perceive this very clearly, if we imagine ourselves visiting the poor at home. We can well understand how awkward we should feel without a command of our own language, how unable to comfort, to encourage, or to reprove them, how utterly at a loss to convey the expression of our kind intentions towards them, and our sympathy with them. We should be so constrained by the consciousness of our inability to benefit them as we desired, that we should be tempted to avoid visiting them altogether, or if we did so, from a sense of duty, we should experience no genuine satisfaction in our employment. Now it is easy to draw the parallel, for it is precisely so, that we are situated in India, without an adequate knowledge of the language of the people among whom we are labouring. We must, therefore, lay it down as a principle on our arrival, that we will allow nothing to divert us from the study of the native tongue, until we have acquired a sufficient knowledge of it to do thus much.

I may here remark in passing, that a single lady coming out has an advantage over a married one, in the greater leisure and freedom from interruption she will enjoy for study; and on this account one might be inclined to advocate the engagement of single ladies in missionary work, as they may thereby become better fitted for the sphere they have to fill, before they are involved in domestic duties. It may certainly be urged against this, that a lady will, perhaps, after having acquired the language of one province, be called to settle finally in a part of the country where a different one is spoken. We believe, however, that conscientious and devoted females, possessing strong principle, would either hesitate in making such a change, or else would do so only under the conviction, that from a similarity between the languages, they could easily acquire that of the province to which they removed. Of course the acquisition of one oriental language is always in some degree a help to the attainment of another, and most if not all of the languages spoken by Hindus in the northern parts of India, (I except Hindusthanie, which is the language of the Mussulmans) are dialects derived from the Sungskrit, so that there is a great deal of connection between them.

A benevolent disposition must be in active exercise, for the duties and kind offices we should be willing to perform, if necessary, for those around us (though I would not give the idea that we shall be constantly called upon to do such things) are sometimes, from the nature of the climate, the habits of the people, as opposed to our own, and other circumstances to which reference is needless, unpleasant in the extreme, and nothing but real genuine benevolence reconciles the mind to discharge them. I have seen a European, who would have been shocked to be charged with want of feeling, allow a poor native to die, when humanly speaking, life might have been saved by timely interference, which nothing but disgust prevented him from rendering. That I do not allude to a missionary, or to a pious person, will readily be supposed; but I am convinced from my own experience, that this feeling often operates, even upon *us*, more strongly than we are aware of, for I have repeatedly detected myself shrinking from duties, that I am sure would have excited no repugnance at home. The disgusting and revolting customs of heathenism produce an effect on the mind, to which a truly benevolent disposition will prove the best counterpoise.

I come now to speak of the religious character, and those qualities more immediately connected with it, and flowing from it. I wish I were capable of doing any thing like justice to this part of my subject, upon which all the other parts hinge and turn; but here I especially feel my weakness and inability, and the need of being taught how to write. I would premise, that the piety of a missionary female must be deep and strong, rather than outwardly enthusiastic or striking; not unlovely and repulsive, but pure and gentle, majestic and amiable, favourable alike to the enjoyment and communication of happiness. It is no common measure of piety we need, and no small degree of devotedness of spirit that will carry us through our trying and arduous course. Our faith must be pre-eminently strong, for it will encounter constant discouragements. It must be of that nature that regards a doubting and wavering disposition as a dangerous foe to our progress, and as far as respects ourselves or our work, especially a sin. The "same mind must be in us which was also in Christ Jesus," who "made himself of no reputation," notwithstanding his inherent greatness and majesty. *He* must be our pattern, and we must bear his image outwardly and inwardly. Our meekness, patience, gentleness, and other christian graces must shine out brightly, for we are truly "as a city set on a hill," that cannot be hid, and all these will have to be in daily exercise. With clear and distinguishing perceptions of what true piety is, and what it requires, and with a settled, well-grounded assurance of our own personal interest in Christ's redemption, there must exist a heart warm with love to Him, a lively and abiding sense of his fulness and sufficiency, of the excellence and truth of the promises of his Word, with correct views of our utter helplessness and dependence upon Him. We should also possess a strong and impelling desire to do whatever the Lord requires, a willingness to give up comforts and submit to privations, to forsake ease and endure toil, to change the society of friends for that of enemies, and to make every sacrifice of personal gratification, for the one great object of promoting the knowledge of Christ.

I believe that none can understand, but those who have been made to do so from experience, the deadening influence of a residence among heathens upon one's moral and spiritual nature. It seems, as it were, to harden the heart's best affections. We need, from our peculiar position, to be living ever in the atmosphere of prayer, whereas an almost irresistible influence appears to be using all its force to destroy devotional habits and feelings. We can enter into the apostle's meaning when he said, "We wrestle not against flesh and blood, but against principalities, and powers, and the rulers of the darkness of this world." One would naturally think, when contemplating the miseries of heathenism in our own christian land, that the nearer approach to and view of them, would increase our zeal and our earnestness tenfold, but this is not the usual effect of it. The prince of the power of the air reigns with a spiritual force in India that is quite indescribable; and I have heard the remark repeatedly from the best missionaries, that when standing in or near heathen temples, and beholding the abominations of heathen worship, while feeling on the one hand the strongest inward impulse to testify against these things, they have been conscious at the same time of such a repelling influence, that it has required the most determined effort, in the strength of the Lord, "to cry out, and lift up their voice" before the multitude, on behalf of the truth. India is not more emphatically a land of bright and glorious sunshine, than it is a land of moral "darkness that may be felt." It is (like Pergamos) the place "where Satan's seat is," and "where Satan dwelleth." (Rev. ii. 13.) Need I prove, then, that if we want piety, if we want faith, if we want prayer, as members of a christian community at home, we require all these in a much greater proportion in a heathen country, and these we must take with us, and not expect to obtain them there. These we must maintain, with a determined energy and perseverance that only the Lord can impart. So shall we be enabled to labour for Him, and to wrestle with Him for the heathen, as well as to keep up his communion in our own souls.

I have thus attempted, my dear friend, to give you some faint idea of the description and degree of piety missionary females need, to enable them to sustain it against all the shocks to which it is subjected, and the unfavourable circumstances under which it has to develop itself. Our piety must not be, as I have heard it strikingly expressed, the piety of the church, the piety of feeling, needing the helps of our fellow Christians, of our pastors, of our sanctuary services, and the other enjoyments and privileges of a christian land to keep it in vigorous exercise; no, what we want is spirituality, personal holiness, and a real and practical regard of the Lord Christ as our Master. This kind of piety will shine brightest and stand firmest when all outward helps and excitements are removed; for it can only result from the work of the Spirit within us, and from his love and grace possessing us, and this is abiding, and will last us in the time of need and extremity. Well may we here pause to enquire, "Who is sufficient for these things?" Only those who can say with Paul, "I can do all things through Christ which strengtheneth me." "Yet not I, but the grace of God which is in me." Only those who believe, that He who commandeth us, "Be ye perfect, as your Father who is in heaven is perfect," and who "knows our works and our labours," will stand at our right hand, to sustain and to help us, to quicken and to encourage us, to make us "faithful unto death," that we may receive "the crown of life." Out of his fulness shall we ever receive grace in addition to grace.

The heart warms at the thought, that in this blessed work of missions, female piety has in several instances, and may yet again in more, recover and display anew the glory which it won, when it poured costly ointment on the Saviour's head, when it wept at his cross, and was early at his sepulchre.

Springing from piety such as I have tried to pourtray will be christian modesty, that beautiful ornament to all women, and that very essential one to the exalted position occupied by the female missionary labourer. Retiredness will follow, though it might seem at first sight, almost incompatible with the circumstances in which such a female is placed. It is not so in fact, for I have seen the most devoted and useful among us exemplify it most remarkably, and the *spirit* of retiredness is always attainable, though a certain degree of publicity may be involved in the profession we sustain. Study humility,—pray for humility,—be humble, said a dear missionary to a young female friend in parting. The humble attract the regard of those who cannot always duly estimate the principle from which true humility springs; and humility preserves tenderness and susceptibility of heart, keeps the spirit near the Saviour, and is therefore, one of the greatest helps to success in missionary work. "Be ye clothed with humility."

I will reserve my remarks on some other qualifications, as a good judgment, an aptitude for teaching, &c., to a future letter, when I shall have to refer more particularly to the characteristics desirable for a missionary's wife, as this is already long enough. Habitual earnestness in all we undertake, counting the cost, and weighing the difficulties, but still persevering in the task, assured that the end to be attained will repay us for every effort we make; is the disposition we should cultivate. This evinces a greatness of mind that cannot be appalled or disturbed by trifles, and that will feel its ardour only quickened by hindrances and obstructions.

In conclusion let me add, that as the three grand qualities for a missionary are said to be decision, devotedness, and perseverance, so these in the female labourer must be softened by the possession of much christian meekness; for where the first exist too strongly in woman, she cannot be "lovely, as well as of good report;" and where the latter prevails without the former, she can hardly be said to be pre-eminently fitted for the high and holy sphere in which she is called to move.

Yours, &c.

M. W.

LETTER IV.

ON THE DOMESTIC CHARACTER OF A MISSIONARY'S WIFE.

My dear Friend,

I HAVE thought it better to devote a letter entirely to this subject, because it requires, in many respects, quite a distinct consideration from the *general* character, and qualifications of a missionary female labourer, and my earnest desire is to elucidate every point you wish to be informed on, fully in all its bearings—though I would guard against tediousness and repetition very carefully.

All that may be said and urged from the Word of God, upon the duty and particular sphere of wives, in every position, applies with increased force to one occupying so elevated a standing in the church as a missionary's wife—this will be fully conceded by all who take a right view of missionary responsibility at large. I will therefore proceed at once to notice those characteristics, which should shine out the strongest, and those qualifications which should be possessed most fully, by one bearing the name of a helpmeet to a missionary.

A cheerful contented spirit should be her outward adornment, maintained against that peculiar tendency to melancholy induced by an Indian climate, which even affects the Hindus as a nation. Perhaps in no country can we more fully estimate the truth of the apostle's assertion, "that godliness *with contentment*, is great gain," than in India, and a cheerful contented spirit is so well calculated to exercise a beneficial influence on ourselves, our households, and our partners, that is worthy of our best efforts for its acquirement and maintenance.

I have seen more than one instance of excellent and devoted missionaries being rendered quite unhappy, and in a great measure unfitted for their duties—not because they had not pious and devoted wives, but because they had wives of a sad and melancholy cast of mind, who yielded to habitual depression, and I have often thought, that if there be one thing of an outward nature, that we should strive after and pray for more than another, it should be a uniformly cheerful contented spirit under all circumstances. Nothing can so effectually help us to take a happy view of untoward and discouraging events, and to bear the various weaknesses and bodily inconveniences, almost or quite inseparable from a hot climate, without being overwhelmed by them ; and nothing can better promote that calmness and serenity so needful to a close and intimate communion with God.

A diligent activity must be observed,—for time is with us a precious commodity, and one which we need most carefully to redeem. "Whatsoever thy hand findeth to do, do it with all thy might," seems a peculiarly binding injunction, in a country where it often happens that "In the morning we flourish, and in the evening we are cut down, and withered." I do not mean by this a bustling busy restlessness, that only tends to expend the strength, and in a great degree to hinder, rather than further, the actual, regular, discharge of duties—but that quiet, unapparent sort of activity, not consisting altogether in bodily motion, but in an ever-present readiness and preparedness to fulfil each engagement with promptitude, in its proper time and place, and in accustoming oneself to the *habit* of attending to every call without unnecessary delay.

By this means much of our own, and of our husband's valuable time is saved, while *his* comfort is thereby better secured, for such diligence involves punctuality at meals, and in all other household arrangements, in which he and our families are concerned and connected as well as ourselves.*

* It may be interesting to the general reader to sketch the employments of a day, though the minutiæ of the arrangements may not apply to all, yet it will give some idea of the routine of our engagements as missionaries' wives.

At sun rise, after securing the morning's retirement, go out, and look round the garden, giving directions to the gardener, and proceed to the Infant and other School to observe, that all is commenced in time and going on in order. Ask a few questions of the children indiscriminately, and suggest any thing that may strike you.—Return to the house, examine and direct the bathing and dressing of the children, just come in from their morning airing—dress yourself and give

To be thoughtful both for others and ourselves is important, guarding with all due

the children their breakfast.—When your husband returns from his preaching, sit down to breakfast, and immediately after, proceed to the store room, and with the assistance of the girl training in that department, weigh out the articles required for the day, and make them over to the cook, and order the dinner. Then attend to domestic business, after which your presence is very desirable in the School, where the girls are employed from ten till two in needle work, embroidery, &c. with an interval of a quarter of an hour's recreation after twelve. The christian women come during this time to bring home their work and receive directions. Very frequent interruptions occur, as notes and letters must be written occasionally—medicines prepared for the sick—work cut out—and visitors sometimes come in. After dining at two, a little time must be given for rest. At four the girls assemble for afternoon reading, and at five all closes with prayer. Then prepare for a walk or a drive, or a visit to a native christian family; return to tea at seven, when your husband comes in from evening preaching. After tea the children go to bed, and the time is employed in reading, writing, or sewing, and on moonlight nights in visiting the native christian families in their cottages, or the orphan school to give the girls a little address. After family prayer at nine, retire.

precaution the health and comfort of those under our influence. I have heard an excellent missionary, whose zeal often tended to lead him beyond the bounds of prudence, say repeatedly, "I believe that, humanly speaking, I should have died long ago, if I had not been married." This spoke much for the judicious, prudent care of his wife, and where *her* heart is, as it ever should be, as devoted and warm with love to God and souls as her husband's, there is no fear of her urging him to undue precaution, or any thing beyond that which prudence requires. We have in this respect a duty t perform, to all who may reside with us, as assistants or otherwise, and we should make it a point of conscience, to use the best means for guarding them against the effects of the climate, in the arrangements of the house, the accommodation, diet, and other particulars.

Our discretion must therefore be equal to our thoughtfulness, and we must endeavour, by our well-ordered establishment, to reflect honour on God, on our husbands, and on our calling, and to set an example to the native christian women, which will influence *them*, more than direct exhortation. This will also not be without its good and happy effect upon the European community, near whom we may be placed, who can mark excellency and discern inconsistency very correctly; particularly in missionaries. This seems a suitable place, though it will be in some sort a digression, for introducing a remark or two upon the kindness we frequently receive from the European families residing near us, which calls for the exercise of discretion in many ways. We may and should be very grateful for attentions shewn to us by them, and regard them as some of the alleviations we are favoured to enjoy in our arduous course; but we must carefully guard against being unduly influenced by such attentions, or allowing them to make us in any measure to forget, as they are perhaps somewhat calculated to do, our position as missionaries to the heathen,—as those who have given up the world, and the things of the world, and who have a higher and holier vocation than that connected with enjoying the favour of superiors, and the fascinating society of the polished and agreeable, among our fellow countrymen.

It is not my intention to recommend entire separation from their society, when they are disposed and desirous to be friendly. We may be able to exercise a good and useful influence over them in many ways, and the pecuniary help they are generally so willing to afford our missions, we ought ever thankfully to receive, acknowledge, and appreciate, as it often considerably extends our ability to prosecute our labours. It is one of the most pleasing features of the times that European society in India really co-operates in many instances, with the more immediate labourers in the work of missions so extensively, that it has been said, that even were missionaries withdrawn from India, it would still enjoy the benefit of a considerable portion of missionary effort. We may be so situated as to find it a great and essential relief to our bodies and spirits occasionally to avail ourselves of intercourse with our neighbours; but all should be within due bounds, which discretion will teach. The case is of course altered, if we are favoured with the vicinity of one or more truly pious families or individuals, who can enter into our feelings, appreciate our labours, understand our trials, and sympathize with us as dearly beloved brethren; but we must not expect this often to occur in a small station, though blessed be God, there are many such persons scattered through the length and breadth of India, whose number is I hope continually augmenting.

It may likewise happen that we shall be placed in some degree of connection with Europeans, from our husbands having to perform spiritual duties for them, in the entire absence of any other means of grace, than those which can be afforded by missionaries. In such case a certain intercourse is indispensable and becomes a duty; but as English ministers become more numerous, and the stations get better supplied with their services, to which end strenuous efforts are now being made by our excellent diocesan, the missionaries will be left more free to their own peculiar work, which fully requires all their zeal, energy, and strength.

Hospitality and kind cordiality should be another prominent feature in a missionary's wife. We have many calls and occasions to practise hospitality in India, from the nature of the country, and our comparatively isolated situation in it, as strangers and foreigners. We cannot look to the natives for the exercise of much of this, because they are prevented from rendering it, by the peculiarities of their religion, and it is therefore a duty for *us* to be prepared and willing to take trouble for each other, and to submit to inconveniences, to serve and assist each other, in a way to which we are not at all called in England. "Use hospitality one to another without grudging. As every one hath received the gift, even so minister the same one to another, as good stewards of the manifold grace of God." 1 Peter iv. 9, 10. I have known a missionary sister have three others in her house at once, who by circumstances were compelled to avail themselves of her hospitality for a length of time, and through illness, which involved much additional labour upon her; and all was cheerfully sustained. Such extreme cases do not often occur, but our hearts and our houses should be always open, and all our means and ability to help each other should be available in times of need, without being permitted to be an unnecessary hindrance to us in our missionary vocation, which it will not be, when it can be left to depend on the wife, and not to interfere with the time and important engagements of the husband. What is this, but giving a practical illustration of that character for denying ourselves, which we should ever be trying to establish, as the point that should be prominent in us, and which is sure to be looked for by others, while so great will be our inward reward and satisfaction, that we shall not be conscious we deny ourselves at all, and it will thus become apparent, that we live only for *one* object, the glory of God, and the good of others.

Simplicity in dress, in household arrangements, and in our general ideas we must studiously practise. From the habits of European society, and from various circumstances peculiar to, and inseparable from a residence in India, one may, when not on one's guard, fall almost unconsciously into a style of management, that does not consist well with a missionary establishment, and though no real or actual extravagance may be practised, an excuse is given to those who delight to act as censors, to exercise their uncharitable remarks, which we should guard against allowing them any opportunity to do. I have often observed, that some things which startle us in others on our arrival, become eventually rather too familiar, and we are in danger of forgetting simplicity altogether. I would be no advocate for unnecessary self-denial of the body—it is both unwise and unsafe. I would have missionaries to enjoy every outward comfort, and every reasonable alleviation to the climate, but the *spirit* of simplicity must prevail, and be apparent all through.

The ability to manage the domestic business of the house well should be an object of solicitude with the missionary's wife, though we have in India servants, to whom, from the nature of the climate, we must entrust the actual performance of it. Yet it is of great importance to possess a thorough knowledge of household economy, that we may be prepared not only to provide for our families every necessary comfort, but to disburse our limited, though sufficient income, in the most profitable way; leaving enough and to spare, for the claims of hospitality and charity. The servants we employ are not of course first rate, and cannot in many instances prepare the little delicacies, which are required for invalids, but when we are able to help ourselves in these matters, we are not left to depend on their ability or inability. Besides this, the native servants are so unprincipled, that one may be ruined without care, even with a large income, and nothing imposes so effectual a check upon their cupidity, as perceiving, which they always do very quickly, whether their mistress understand the minutiæ of domestic business or not. It may perhaps be enquired here, why we do not select christian servants from among the converts? to which I reply, that we do as far as practicable, but as they have seldom been so employed before their conversion, the engagement of christian servants, generally involves a greater necessity for a good knowledge of housewifery on the part of the mistress.

The same style of argument holds good, with respect to the ability to superintend the cutting out and making of linen, garments, children's clothes, &c. The principle of selfishness, so conspicuous in Hindus, teaches them to try to serve and please those most, whom they judge to be the best able to appreciate a degree of faithfulness, and to detect the contrary.

This leads me to speak of the management of our servants, a most difficult part of our duty, whether they be professing Christians or heathens, in the fulfilment of which, "patience" does indeed need to "have her perfect work." Their cheating, lying, pilfering, and deceitful habits, form one of our greatest outward trials, but yet they may be managed, and we may enjoy even comfort from them, by understanding the best way of treating them. We must ever bear in mind that they are our fellow immortals and our fellow sinners, and that they are or have been, sunk into the lowest degradation of moral feeling from their religion. This will induce a certain tenderness and compassion towards them, that will enable us to bear with much that is vexatious and provoking in itself. We should also be very clear and exact in our directions to them, not blaming them for failure in duties, which perhaps, we had not fully explained to them. I have often heard orders given to servants of so confused and incomprehensible a nature, by those who knew little of the language, that I have really wondered that any kind of idea of what was meant could enter their minds at all, and when these intended orders have been imperfectly obeyed, the entire blame was laid upon the servant, when it more justly belonged to the mistress. It is necessary to be very decided and strict with them, saying little, but shewing by our manner, that we require and look for obedience and attention. They are much like children, and require to be treated as such in many respects. We must try to initiate ourselves, as it were, into their modes of thinking, and above all, we must shew them that we care for their souls, endeavouring, by every possible means, to lead *them* also to feel their value.* We read

* A pious lady, who was the wife of a Colonel, once told me that she had reason to believe that the imperfect instructions she had endeavoured to give to her servants had been useful in impressing two or three of them, who confessed to her on their dying

of one missionary's wife whose servants never lived long with her without being converted; and I know another who has been favoured to make impressions on three, two of whom have become consistent members of a christian church, and the third is only prevented by her husband from following their example. We need, in every department we have to fill, much love to souls. *Love* must be with us the constantly moving principle, such love as Paul felt when he said, "The love of Christ constrains me;" such love as glowed in Jesu's bosom, when He exclaimed, "I lay down my life for the sheep." Not merely

beds, that their hope for salvation was founded on Jesus Christ, and not on their own idols and false refuges.

Another lady, who was very indefatigable and persevering in persuading her household to become Christians, made such an impression on them generally, that one of them who heard a missionary preaching on the universal depravity of man, assured him that he knew one instance to which this truth did not apply, "for my lady," said he, "is entirely perfect." When questioned as to his reason for his assertion, he touchingly related her self-devotedness and love to her servants, but especially her care for their souls.

a sense of duty, however strong, can carry us through, it is *love*, that impelling principle, which must ever be in active exercise. Oh that I could represent this

> "In thoughts that breathe,
> And words that burn."

And if our servants require patience and forbearance to be distinguishing qualities with us, the same are no less needed for our assistants and helpers in our schools, &c. We are, in this respect, beset by peculiar difficulties little understood in a christian land, where if one person do not suit well, we can easily make an exchange, and find others ready to come to us. In India, as far as my experience has gone, I must say, that we have *first* much trouble to procure any thing like really efficient helpers; and when we succeed so far, they often differ in many important particulars from what we could desire; yet, if we find in them but a certain degree of fitness, ability, and willingness to do their best, we may be very thankful, and must gladly train them and bear with them. Very often it will happen that just as they are becoming valuable to us, circumstances occur to deprive us of their services, and we have the same work to do over again with others.

We shall find need to exercise forbearance to our fellow labourers likewise, as we must be conscious they have to do towards us. "Bear ye one another's burdens," said the apostle, "and thus fulfil the law of Christ." We cannot expect that those with whom we are associated will be, in all cases, kindred spirits, though they may be excellent and devoted co-workers. Sometimes the very reverse may be the case; and it should therefore be our aim to be no less conspicuous for consistency ourselves, than for tenderness towards the failings and short comings of others. We must remember that, as women, "our strength is in our influence," and on us it greatly depends to maintain that spirit of unanimity and cordiality so extremely desirable among missionary brethren. Never should we indulge in speaking of any defects *we* may feel and observe in them, for it is not what we *think* of a person, but what we *say* of him, that injures him in our own opinions and in the eyes of others: and a mischievous tattling is, of all sources, one of the most fruitful, in producing sad misunderstandings and heart-burnings; not less among missionaries than amongst other Christians.

A good judgment is an invaluable qualification for a missionary's wife, and the want of it will cause a lamentable failure in many of her plans, while the possession of it will make her an additionally valuable helpmeet to her husband, who will often be glad of her advice, her counsels, her cautions, and her encouragements. That quickness of perception, facility of adaptation, and acuteness of feeling, peculiar to woman, eminently fit her to become an acquisition to her husband, when these are tempered with a judgment, on the soundness of which he can rely. She will know, if she has this, when to come forward, and when to withdraw, and will be preserved from interfering in matters which do not belong to her sphere, and with respect to which she should be very guarded.

Much harm and many painful feelings often arise from females aiming at a kind and degree of authority and influence that do not belong to them. It seems to me out of character for us to come forward spontaneously, with our advice and opinions on important matters, connected perhaps with the management of the mission, in the presence of the other sex, unless we are expressly solicited to do it. "If any man offend not in word, the same is a perfect man," saith the apostle; and this is a kind of perfection it well becomes us to strive after, yea, which it is a duty for us to aim at.

"We never listen to what Mrs. —— says," remarked a missionary to me one day, "though she always gives us her ideas as to the points, upon which she hears us conversing in our conferences. We just wait till she ceases to speak, and then resume the subject where she interrupted it." What a reproof ought this to have been to the individual in question, who was one least calculated to give a judicious and useful opinion, and who, if she had not been so, most effectually hindered herself from being invited to do it, by her forwardness.

If a husband has reason to value his wife's judgment, he will always apply to her in private, where she will feel more at liberty to speak to, and advise him freely and openly, according to the best of her ability.

A missionary's wife must be ready with her plans for *seizing* every opening for usefulness, and in this way *she* will see many means, that would escape the observation of others. It is by this tact in catching at opportunities, that eminent usefulness may be attained. A fertility for planning, and an energy to carry out such designs as appear likely to promote good, in connection with a sound judgment, will be of service.

A natural tact for training up children, is most desirable, not only as enabling us to conduct our schools efficiently, but as fitting us for the due discharge of our maternal duties, in which we shall not generally enjoy the helps that are available at home. It will depend almost entirely on ourselves individually, to manage and instruct our little ones, and this duty we have to perform surrounded by a host of hindrances, inseparable from a missionary life in a heathen country. It is true that in most instances our children must be removed from us after a few years, and sent to suitable care in a christian land, but so long as they are with us, all the above remarks apply. Happy is it for us that we are permitted the privilege of influencing their infant years, though deprived of the gratification of completing their training, and subjected to the sad and sore affliction of a long and perhaps final separation from them. I cannot but embrace this opportunity for remarking, that while we have our children with us, we should make an effort to impress on their minds the deep importance of the work in which their parents are engaged, so as to bias their affections and desires in favour of it; or if they leave us too soon for *us* to do this, we should try and select a home for them among those, who we feel confident will best fulfil *our* place in this respect, by endeavouring, so to speak, to educate them for future service in our place.* It has often

* How much do missionaries owe to those dear christian friends, who have organized such institutions as the school for missionaries' daughters at Walthamstow, which is intended for those of different denominations among Dissenters. Could not a similar school be set on foot for the daughters of Church missionaries? There seems something peculiarly appropriate and interesting, in the idea of missionaries' children being educated *together*, and in a separate institution.

excited surprise that so few of the children of missionaries have entered upon mission work, when they grew up, and it does seem remarkable, and a subject for regret. If we are real missionaries at heart, and living in our work, there is nothing we shall desire more strongly, next to the conversion of our children to God, than that they should become devoted and useful labourers, in the same blessed employment, to which we have dedicated our own lives.

In all respects a missionary's wife must be a careful woman, and yet she must be "without carefulness," and guard against undue anxiety, remembering the apostolic injunction, to "be careful for nothing, but in *every* thing, by prayer and supplication, to make her requests known unto God."

This leads me to refer to that characteristic, which must crown every other. She must be *emphatically a prayerful woman*, for "prayer is influence: prayer moves heaven, and all other things become prayerful only through prayer." She must "pray without ceasing;" be ever lifting up her heart to God in devout desires. She must feel the invitation, "Come my people, enter into your chamber," as addressed especially to *her*, for if prayer is, as has been said, the pulse of a Christian, it must more particularly be regarded as the pulse of a missionary.

Her own soul needs prayer—her husband—her children—the mission—the converts—the heathen—and the brethren, need it. Her spirit should be deeply devotional. The characteristic perseverance of the woman, by which she can be so useful to man, should in this be very apparent; then what a help will she prove to her husband in private, and what a blessing to her sphere at large, for the amount of the influence of fervent persevering prayer can never be told. It is not by natural "might nor by power, but by my Spirit, saith the Lord," that the heathen are to be converted, and we are to help forward their conversion. And how are we to obtain the Spirit's help without diligently seeking it? "If we look into the censer of the angel standing at the golden altar which is before the throne," and if we there "mark what it is of all human instrumentality which ascends to heaven, we shall find that it is only that which is sanctified by *prayer*—only that which partook of the nature of prayer. This is all that lives to reach the skies; all that is ever permitted," of our poor service to ascend before God. Many who were active and zealous before men, will be left "comparatively unnoticed," in the great day, while the humble female, who wrestled with God, and thereby brought down his blessing upon those with whom she was associated, as perhaps the most seemingly insignificant among them, will be drawn out from her closet obscurity, and proclaimed in their stead, for it will then appear, that while they were moving only *earth*, *she* was moving *heaven*. Jesus, our great Intercessor, who ever liveth to plead with and for us, will never hold *his* peace, till the righteousness of Zion go forth as brightness, and the salvation of Jerusalem as a lamp that burneth, nor must we hold our's, if we wish to be efficient labourers. No—we must neither "keep silence," nor give the Father "rest," till we feel that we have no more needs for ourselves or others; and this can never be, "till mortality is swallowed up of life," and prayer is exchanged for praise. I cannot well restrain my pen on this subject.

I feel that few, perhaps none of us, pray enough, and I would that something I could say, stirred us up to a more general conviction of our privileges in this respect, for we as *wives* seem particularly called to prayer and all private efforts, as our husbands are to preaching and public ones. Oh that every one of us might be enabled so to cultivate this duty, as to be able to say as a dear sister (now departed) said to her husband, "*thousands* of prayers have I offered for you, since I have been your's!" Missionaries are continually giving, as it were, and never receiving, and when they return home, weary and worn out from their exhausting labours, then do they need to enjoy the soothing tones of prayer, which assure them, that if *it* can prevail with God, their labours shall not be in vain; then do they need to have their spirits, depressed with the heat, cheered by references to that blessed land, where "the sun shall smite" no more, and to those sweet gospel consolations, which can only be suggested by her who dwells continually near the life-giving fountain, and like a stream flowing forth from it, refreshes the region it passes through.

The sufficiency of the Saviour's grace and strength is made perfect in weakness; and the wife, though "the weaker vessel," may be by her prayers, a real strengthener of her husband's faith, and a great helper of his joy. She can thus "bear his burdens," bring down success to his labours, enlighten his path, and help to keep alive the fire of heaven upon the altar of his heart. Not one true prayer can ever be lost; but the faintest and humblest petition, offered in faith, adds something to those treasures of grace which are kept in reserve for the supply of all our future needs; and which, when they have accumulated to a certain fulness, will be poured out in all their plenitude upon us individually, upon the church, and upon the world at large.

There is one more point on which I must touch, which though it comes last, is not the least important, for it refers to a subject that greatly involves our usefulness in all the others yet considered. A missionary's wife must be a woman of a catholic spirit. As missionaries, we are not labourers for this or that particular section of the church, but we are servants of the Lord Jesus Christ, irrespective of any other master. We should strive to divest ourselves of any thing like party spirit, and to view religion in its primitive amplitude, before it was broken into parties, and clogged with the inventions of men. *Our* business is *only* to make known the truth of the Gospel; and, perhaps, a greater amount of blessing has been withheld from missionary labour on account of our losing sight of this, than many might suppose or like to allow. As the servants of a party, we have no right to hope that *He* to whom all sections of his church are equally dear, *can* bless us, for He makes us no promise to encourage us to do so; but "as workers together" with *Him*, we must and shall be blessed. And if we can but feel ourselves to be such, and only such,—regarding and duly appreciating the *spiritual* nature of our work; cultivating that compassion and love to all, that made David weep "rivers of water," and turned Jeremiah's "eyes into a fountain of tears," that caused the beloved Redeemer himself to sorrow over Jerusalem, and the apostolic Paul to wish himself accursed for his brethren, we shall feel no disposition to undervalue and despise the labours of *any* of the Lord's servants, engaged in the same all-glorious work of winning the heathen to Christ;—no, we shall rejoice in their success, and sympathize in their disappointments and trials, in the same measure as in our own. Such a spirit will help our prayers, and our exertions, and fill our hearts and minds with peace, that peace which springeth from *love;* and we shall thus give our converts and the heathen the benefit of seeing,—what will have a more powerful effect on them than any thing else—how we all as "Christians love one another." Emulations and strifes will cease, and the Spirit of Christ our common Head will exemplify itself in our daily conduct. In this respect, as I have remarked before, *our* strength is in our influence, and *we*, as females, exercise an unseen but strong power over the entire circle in which we move.

Perhaps some will say the character drawn out is unattainable; but I have been privileged to see, by a practical exemplification of it, that it is not; and excellence that has been attained by the few, may be attained by the many. Only let every christian sister who may read this letter, be incited to pray more for us. Only let every one, perceiving what we ought to be, and how much grace we must receive to help us—only let them remember, that we have the same weaknesses and infirmities as our fellow-believers; and then, I hope *they* will see and feel too, how much it depends on *them*, as well as on ourselves, whether we shall reach the standard I have laid down or not. Far be it from me to hold up missionary wives to the *admiration* of the church; for in going out to labour among the heathen, they do no more than their duty to Him who has done so much for them. They make no sacrifice adequate to what his love deserves; for correctly speaking, the world has had but *one* sacrifice (*i. e.* that of Christ himself,) and can never have another, that is worthy of the name in comparison with *that;* but to the sympathy and prayers of the church they have an especial claim, and for this I venture earnestly to plead.

Yours, &c.

M. W.

LETTER V.

ON THE PREPARATION NECESSARY FOR ENGAGING IN MISSIONARY WORK.

My dear Friend,

PERHAPS some may smile at the idea suggested by the heading of this letter, as it has not, I am told, been customary in England in the majority of cases, for females who become united to missionaries, to be led to consider it necessary to prepare themselves for missionary work.

Those who have gone out single, have I believe generally undergone some degree of preparation, extending to the acquisition of the most approved school systems; but this, as far as relates to the mechanical part of them, they have not found of much practical use to them on their arrival in India.

Our most useful labourers have been those

whom natural character, and previous providential discipline have prepared, and this is undoubtedly the best and most important preparation, and that for which no other can adequately compensate, although it does not render all other unnecessary. As however, not every one who may be called to enter the missionary field, will or can be even thus prepared, it becomes a matter for consideration whether we should not do wisely, in the case of women, as in that of men, to allow them the opportunity for such preparation as may seem best calculated to fit them for greater usefulness, and more active exertions than they would otherwise be likely to attain and accomplish.

I have heard that, in America, very considerable attention is paid to this particular, but whether generally and upon system, or only in occasional instances, I cannot say. We have however, some striking examples of the peculiar fitness of certain individuals among the American females for missionary labour, as Mrs. Judson, Mrs. Winslow, and others, and I am convinced from what I have seen of them, that they have either been selected with more reference to the station they have to occupy than our own countrywomen, or have, after their selection, undergone some particular preparation for it.*

It will not appear unnatural or unreasonable to any who will take the subject into serious consideration, that a character such as has been described in the preceding letter, will not generally be found perfectly qualified to enter upon the arduous and trying path of a female labourer in a heathen land, without a period spent in preparation for it.

At one time little importance was attached to the idea of men going out as missionaries, being required to be prepared, in any other way than by possessing extreme devotedness; but now we all allow, that they

* Since publishing the first edition of these letters, I have met with and perused, a Memoir of Mrs. Margaret Wilson of Bombay, and I take this opportunity of remarking, that she appears to me a model for all missionaries' wives. I would strongly recommend the study of her character and devoted course of labour to all females who contemplate missionary work.

must pass many years in study, and in disciplining their minds for their anticipated duties; and although quite a different and a much less extensive preparation is required for the female, yet if she is to fulfil her sphere well, which is in its place as important as his, why must she be expected to do so without any of the preparatory aids he has enjoyed? Do not mistake me, or imagine, for a moment, that I aim to put woman on an equality with man; for I am quite conscious of the point on which she is and ought to be content to be his inferior, *i. e.* in mental power,—but in excellence and fitness for her appointed duties, it is no presumption for her to aim at equality, and this is all I mean to recommend. I fear our standard (if we have had one) has hitherto been too low on this head; we have considered, that if a woman had but true piety, and a devoted heart, all the rest would follow as a matter of course: but it is not so, and if we exercised our common sense a little, we should never imagine it would be so.

We can all perceive, and understand fully, that a pastor's wife at home should be a superior woman, and one of no common character and attainments; or at least we can see that if she is such, she will exercise much more influence, and be likely to do much more good, than if she be a mere commonplace person; though it may be, not wanting in true piety, and devotedness of heart. Does not the parallel hold good with increased force, when it is drawn with regard to the wife of a missionary, who has a more prominent and conspicuous post to fill, and a more difficult work to accomplish, and greater trials and discouragements to bear up under? Assuredly it does. Naturally and by preparation she should be a superior character; and if she is so, we may reasonably hope, that she will do a greater amount of good, than she could be expected to do otherwise. Her husband will be better advised, her family better trained, her household better managed, her schools better conducted, and the whole apparatus of the mission better arranged, than is possible when no adequate fitness exists in one, who must from her position, be a moving spirit.

Hitherto we have had so many difficulties

in the way, as it regards our efforts among the native females, that it might have been considered, however erroneously, as of little importance how qualified the missionaries' wives were for usefulness, so long as they could just be a comfort and a solace to their husbands; for it was often said, even by missionaries, that no public sphere existed for at least the majority of them. Now however, that things are coming into a better and more promising train, this cannot so well be urged. Our orphans, the children of our native congregations, and the adult christian females, form a sufficient employment for all our energies and powers, however great they may be, and when we are stationed in places where these do not exist, various other occupations, requiring ability and superiority of mind;—such as translations and preparations of books suitable for our pupils, which are daily felt to be a greater desiderata, will not be wanting, to say nothing of the *additional* help and comfort a suitable and superior wife can be to her husband, in various ways that it is not here in place to point out. I know I have heard *many* lament over their experienced inability very feelingly; but I never heard one of the most gifted say, or even infer the idea, that she considered herself too competent or too well suited to her sphere. No, all, even the best, have felt their want of greater fitness, greater ability, greater aptness, and better preparedness than they were conscious of possessing.

Many after reading these remarks may still continue to smile at my idea; but if what I have said cannot be disproved, then I am on the right side, and may proceed to speak of the kind of preparation that seems desirable, and the time that should be occupied in it, and allowed for it; the duration of which must in a great measure depend upon the degree of fitness previously possessed by those whose minds become directed towards the missionary field, as their future location.

The preceding letters have enumerated the qualifications that are desirable for a missionary female; and it will be easy for all who have read them with attention, to judge for themselves respecting the preparation best calculated to assist in forming such a character as has been depicted.

We must take it for granted that the individual in question has been endued by the God of nature with a good degree of ability, and by the God of grace with a large measure of piety and zeal, and here we have our ground-work. It will occur in some, and I would fain hope in many cases, that a thoroughly good solid education has been received in youth, and that the mind has been well formed for useful labours and exertions in *any* sphere, for such, of course, a comparatively slight degree of preparation is required; and this will consist chiefly in endeavouring to increase the information, especially as it respects missionary work, and the training of children, and in perfecting herself in all kinds of useful and domestic knowledge, with pursuing a simple course of theological reading, under a friend capable of conducting her through it. The study of the language might perhaps be begun in England, and continued on the voyage, but no great progress will be made in this, in most cases, till a residence among the people help it forward.

But there may be others, though we would hope not the majority, who from not having enjoyed the early advantages of the former, will find it desirable to spend a longer time in, and to use much more vigorous means of preparation.

Such as have either been imperfectly or but superficially educated, should diligently apply themselves to making up for previous disadvantages.

These should resolutely sit down and patiently study, till they can write with as much ease, and feel as well able to express themselves with propriety and correctness in conversation, as if they had been favoured with early instruction: and until their minds are brought into such a state of forwardness, that they are conscious of being prepared to avail themselves of, and to profit by, every future opportunity of improvement that may be offered. This will chiefly be attained by a regular course of well selected reading, under the direction of some able and judicious adviser, and will occupy a year or two, as circumstances may determine.

With regard to acquiring the routine of school systems, as they are carried out at home, I have before said, that merely the mechanical part of these avails but little in India. A natural tact for training and instructing children, and an orderly mind, with ability to plan and arrange, will give every one their own system, which must be adapted to the peculiarities of the climate and the circumstances of the people. Still I would say, make yourself familiar with all that is approved as excellent in the large model schools at home, because, although just the mechanical part may not stand one in much stead, the enlargement of ideas which will be received thereby will be very valuable to us. I need only allude here, having sufficiently referred to it before, to the desirableness of learning to sing well.

There is one point on which I wish to offer a few remarks, and I can do it nowhere better than in this place. When a young woman is about to quit England, for engagements in a heathen land, it is common for friends and relations to desire visits, and in the prospect of her soon leaving her native country, and that in such a cause, she is treated with extraordinary affection and indulgence, too often perniciously flattered, and unconsciously rising in self-esteem, just at a juncture, when if ever in her life, she needs to be overwhelmed with humility and a deep consciousness of her peculiar weakness. In this way, perhaps many valuable weeks and months are spent, and though it is all perfectly natural, it is neither wise nor judicious—it excites a spirit of religious dissipation especially in some dispositions, and helps to undiscipline the mind; which from the very hour that the determination is decidedly formed to devote itself to missionary work, should be subjected to a regular course of training, and habituated to self-denial, particularly mental self-denial, as distinct from bodily. We may visit, and bid friends farewell, but should be very jealous of spending too much time in this way, unless indeed we go to those who can aid us in our preparation, which quite alters the state of the case.

It may not be amiss to suggest here, that in cases where the pecuniary circumstances of the individual to be prepared for missionary work, do not allow of her giving up her time for the necessary period, pious families well disposed to the cause, who have the means and ability, might perhaps sometimes offer a home to her for a year or two, and afford her all the facilities in their power in her preparations. Great good might be done in this way for missions, especially by single ladies, living a quiet and retired life. I have known of one such instance, which led me first to think of the plan.

A very useful means of preparation for every one, would be to engage, for a few weeks or months, in the actual teaching of a large village school, and thus practically learn the fag of training children, who would be the nearest in resemblance (though still superior) to the class we have to labour amongst in India, that could well be found in England. Nothing prepares so well as real experience, and it strikes me that that which could be attained in this manner, in the course of some months personal devotedness, during, say one half of the day, leaving the other half at leisure for study and mental cultivation, would be found very valuable, far more so than simply visiting, and occasionally examining a school, for even a much longer period.

A mind disciplined and prepared as I have described, if a due measure of health and strength be enjoyed, will be found well fitted for usefulness, and may at once undertake the care of a field already under cultivation, or should no such opening present, might safely enter on the more arduous work of breaking up the fallow ground.

Yours, &c.

M. W.

LETTER VI.

ON THE DIFFICULTIES AND TRIALS CONNECTED WITH MISSIONARY WORK.

My dear Friend,

Our various trials and difficulties have been necessarily alluded to in an indirect way several times, in the course of the preceding letters; but as this is a part of my subject, which is, I know, very imperfectly understood in England, and which I believe it to be of the utmost importance to state clearly and plainly, I will try faithfully to depict our difficulties somewhat in detail, as they are connected with the change in our situation, the climate, the language, and the want of suitable books;—the habits of the people, their division into castes, their apathy, the degraded state of the female population at large, with the low state of moral and spiritual feeling, even among many of the converts.

There are certain experiences that must be felt to be understood, as I have elsewhere had occasion to remark, and these hardly admit of elucidation in writing. The first head I have named above partakes much of this nature, involving as it does, a complete alteration in all our outward circumstances. In going out single this must be more sensibly felt than in going out married; for in the latter case, our home, or at least the centre of it, is with us; but in the former case, one is emphatically *alone*, and a consciousness of *loneliness* must ever accompany us, however kind and sympathizing friends and fellow labourers may be.

To the lady who goes out single, my remarks must chiefly apply, and I would write as if earnestly addressing her personally, and entreat her to ponder deeply over the enquiries that follow, especially if she is surrounded at home by affectionate parents and an attached family circle, loving and being beloved.

Can I endure to be *alone?*—Not alone

actually, but alone as it were in spirit; alone as it regards intimate converse and communion with my nearest and dearest ties; with those who can enter into all my feelings, and make the kindest allowances for all my peculiarities, and to whom I have from childhood been accustomed to look for help and encouragement in my difficulties and distresses. And if she think she can endure this, and will feel the presence of the "Friend that sticketh closer than a brother" sufficient to compensate for the absence of all others, let her again enquire—am I prepared to submit to the peculiarities of those with whom I may have to reside? They may be excellent, devoted people, but not such as I should have selected, or exactly such as I imagine, or at all like those with whom I have hitherto been associated. There may exist some singularity in manner, or some infirmity of disposition, which will affect my comfort and try my temper and patience. Can I endure this? endure it daily, and with probably few changes in the monotony of my usual employments, to make me unconscious or forgetful of it? I wish to suppose a case that may occur, and that sometimes will occur. The young, ardent, and inexperienced, are too apt to regard the "devout men and honourable women," who compose the missionary body, as almost perfect, and not subject to the common failings of other Christians, and this leads them to form erroneous ideas, which often affect them strongly, after they perceive that they have just the same infirmities as others, and perhaps, in some instances, on account of their separation from christian society and other causes, even greater *peculiarities* than are common amongst ministers at home.

And another question, it will be well to ask, is—can I submit to be engaged, day after day, in a work so outwardly uninviting? Not among the charming interesting children imagination often pictures at home, but among *poor degraded heathen*, as wretched in their external appearance as in their internal condition, and as unpromising as can well be conceived, or if not just among these, among those who have but lately been brought out from the midst of them. And then we shall have no excitements, no approving circle to estimate our exertions; none to praise, but many perhaps to find fault; often none who can enter into our motives, or appreciate our perseverance. Can we thus labour on? Oh what disappointments are sometimes seen when a young zealous labourer is first introduced to her future pupils! and need we wonder at this, when one relates that she had been led to imagine her self-denials would consist, in having to eat meat that must be cooked before it had time to cool; and another, that as she would have little good food in India, she had prepared at home by refraining from things she most enjoyed. Such sacrifices would be light, but it is not such; nor is it just one single sacrifice that must be made, and then all be over, but a conduct that involves DAILY sacrifices, and these often of a nature that cannot be appreciated, nor indeed, scarcely be apparent to any but ourselves.

We can form very little idea in England of the overpowering nature of a climate so intensely hot as that of India. Our bodily, mental, and spiritual energies become alike prostrate; and we have to urge ourselves to exertion by the strongest principles. I have however, made considerable allusion to this already, and much enlargement here is therefore unnecessary. We cannot realize ourselves while still in Europe, so situated as to be unable to put our foot out of doors, during the day, without endangering the health or life; and so dependent on others as one must be, not for luxuries, or even exactly for comforts, for these are commodities which, in our English sense of the term, are unknown in tropical climates; but for those necessary alleviations to the great heat, which one must use, to insure a portion of health, and efficiency for the discharge of our duties. What are sometimes incorrectly called luxuries at home, are in fact, only artificial contrivances to obtain some abatement of actual suffering.

It being impossible to go from home during the heat, except in a conveyance, and the weariness produced from the exhaustion of the day being excessive, there exists but little opportunity for visiting the poorer natives, the only class *at all* accessible as heathens; or even for calling on the christian families in their own cottages as we would do in England, except by availing ourselves, with regard to the latter, of moonlight nights, cool evenings after a storm, or such occasional chances. The cautions we need to observe, and the many alleviations we require, place us at a much greater distance from the natives than we would desire to be, and render it more difficult for us to obtain that intimate acquaintance with them in their domestic lives which we would wish.

In speaking thus I have reference chiefly to christian natives, as it will be perceived, when I come to allude to the institution of caste, and to the habits of the people, that there are other and stronger obstacles to intercourse, with regard to the heathen, than even those which the climate impose, but this, in itself, encompasses us with innumerable difficulties on all sides.

The effect that the heat often has upon the health is such, that we become really unequal in many cases, to any great bodily efforts; and with the will, and the most ardent desire, and the real ability to be useful, we are compelled to remain, in a great degree, quiescent.

I have before alluded to the difficulties

connected with the language: and a few brief remarks here will be all that I need make. I wish it to be borne in mind, that we must go out with a determination to conquer *it*, and not to let *it* conquer *us*; and to this end we must study laboriously and diligently while in the ardour of our European or newly arrived strength. It must not be supposed we shall find it so easy to acquire as we found it to learn French or German. The characters; the great difference in the use and value of expression in oriental languages; the domestic and social usages of the people so opposite to our own; their feelings; their ideas; all the very reverse, in many respects, of ours, involve a number of difficulties which we must resolutely set ourselves to surmount in the onset. I am very anxious that our future labourers should, in this respect excel the majority of those who have preceded them, because I feel convinced of the great importance of it, to enable us to do real, solid, permanent good; and in as far as we succeed in overcoming this difficulty we lighten all others; for we shall then be able to instruct our orphans and christian girls with real efficiency, and to train up some of them to be useful hereafter among their own countrywomen, to whom we, as foreigners, can gain no access. We cannot do this entirely by means of English; but as books are prepared, it must be our chief aim to give the most talented and well-disposed among these girls a good education in their own tongue, and only to teach them English, as we learn French or Italian; *i. e.* as an increased means of informing their minds and enlarging their ideas.

The want of suitable books may well be enumerated as another of our difficulties, and one which affords an additional argument for the necessity of an acquaintance with the language, that we may do our part in aiding to prepare them, this I shall refer to again in the succeeding letter.

The hindrances we experience connected with caste, of course apply chiefly to efforts made among the heathen, but still we must be more or less inconvenienced by it in all our labours, till Christianity has made a much more general impression in India, than it can be said to have done at present. It is impossible to explain all the various ways in which it hinders and annoys us, nor is it exactly necessary to do so.*

As far as regards the heathen, it quite prevents us from obtaining any thing like a free and familiar intercourse with Hindu

* We were one evening visiting a native christian family, and after some conversation with them on spiritual subjects, were about to conclude the visit with reading and prayer. We observed the wife leaving the cottage, and taking her place in the verandah, and supposing she could not hear so well there, we begged her to come inside and sit down on a mat with her husband. "I cannot," was her reply. "Why not," we enquired, but she was silent. Her husband then informed us, that as heathens, women were never permitted to sit in the presence of the father-in-law, and though his wife knew *she* was now at liberty to do it, being a Christian, she could not get over early impressions sufficiently to allow her to avail herself of her privilege. We tried to induce her to begin on this occasion, but all our persuasions failed, and she continued outside, while the husband and his father sat together on the mat. When I first came to this station, the christian women were accustomed to sit at church behind the preacher, with their faces to the wall, and it was only by degrees I succeeded in altering this and many other absurd remains of their former usages.

families, by which we might gain access to their affections; friendly, social intimacy is out of the question, for we cannot approach the *domestic* circle, and as the respectable families all live in seclusion, we cannot even so much as see the females. Were it possible for us to visit them as neighbours, to converse with them, to induce them to visit us, and see our schools, the usages of our families, and our christian congregations, much might be done to affect them well towards our religion; but we are entirely debarred through the restrictions imposed by caste, from even attempting to shew those kindnesses which could not fail of making some impression on their hearts, much less can we avail ourselves of the vast influence we might exercise on them by private persuasion in gaining their confidence. All that seems possible at present is, as I remarked above, to train up our most suitable girls with the hope of obtaining access to them hereafter by their means, when every thing with regard to the general establishment of Christianity shall be, as we trust ere long to see it, in a state of greater progress than it now is.

Closely connected with caste are the peculiar habits and customs of the Hindus, so closely indeed that it is sometimes difficult to distinguish between them, for in many respects the latter may be said to spring out of the former, and to impose almost a greater difficulty than it. Their custom of living according to the patriarchal mode in large families, sometimes including four generations under one roof, and the bondage arising from these numerous connections and relatives, any offence against the prejudices of whom, immediately involves them in innumerable troubles, (most difficult to bear, especially for women) deprives them of all independence, both of mind and action, and places them all in habitual subjection to the will of others.

There is no possibility of the females hearing any thing abroad of Christianity, as they are not permitted to go out, and even the lower orders who are abroad, do not think of attempting to intrude themselves into assemblies composed of men, so that preaching must be addressed to the other sex exclusively. The minds of the women are quick and lively, and quite capable of impression, but from the state of society, they are entirely shut out from the opportunity of receiving impressions, so that our work is necessarily confined to christian females, orphans, and our domestic servants. Access in a few instances, but no general access, has yet been gained to the respectable ranks, so that I can think of no other plan with regard to them than the prospective one of preparing some of our orphan girls, with a view of instructing them hereafter.*

A no less serious difficulty arises from the apathy of the general character, or perhaps I should rather say indifference. An excellent and devoted lady, who has made many efforts in

* On one occasion our Infant School was visited by a very rich native gentleman, who had a little girl of his own. He expressed himself exceedingly pleased, and said, "I could not have believed that little Hindu children would have learnt so much." He then enquired whether it would not be possible for him, when his daughter was old enough, to get an instructress for her similar to the young woman I had in the school, who was a Hindu-Briton. This reminds me of the remark of a missionary, who said, "The time is not far distant, when the prejudices, even of the idolatrous natives, shall be so far conquered, that their daughters will be sent to European and Hindu-British females for education."

spite of all hindrances and opposition, to gain occasional access to respectable females, informed me, that their complete indifference to the labour and pains necessary for learning to read, can scarcely be overcome, until their male relatives see it to be so important, as to induce *them* to promote the introduction of efficient plans and regular instruction. There may be a few—I fear it will be found a *very few* exceptions, but the majority, knowing as they do, that there is a much greater dislike than a desire, on the part of their husbands and families to their making any attempt for cultivating their minds, cannot be induced to attempt a persevering effort for it. The same indifference prevails among the lower classes, who, if they may be said to have a choice, would far prefer being left in their ignorance to being taught, and indeed no inducement, but that of gain, and the hope of reward, has hitherto brought them together. Even to the christian females these remarks are in a degree applicable. I have heard of some, but not known any, though I have repeatedly tried it, who could be induced to submit to the drudgery of learning to read when becoming converts after marriage. This is very disheartening to one's spirit, but nothing more can reasonably be expected, considering the nature and tendency of their religion and usages altogether, and it must only lead to the quickening of our own ardour and perseverance.

The degraded state of the female population at large, interposes a difficulty of no ordinary magnitude, and would be fain on its first representation to make us sit down in despair. It is a melancholy picture indeed, but its best effect will be to render us more vigorous in using all the means in our power towards its amelioration, though this must be expected in the natural course of things to be a work of time, and one which can advance but by slow, and almost imperceptible degrees.

From her birth to her death the Hindu female is in an abject condition, being neither permitted to receive education, nor to join in religious duties, such as reading, chanting, and repeating sacred compositions; indeed, with the exception of a very few sentences on morality from the inferior books, it is unlawful for them even to *listen* to such compositions.

It is regarded by the men as disreputable to educate their females, and scarcely two instances can be adduced of persons who have had courage enough to break through the strong current of public feeling, though there is no absolute prohibition against it in the shasters. Then their early marriages, to persons upon whom they are bestowed by their fathers without any previous personal acquaintance, exercise a most baneful influence upon their character in every respect. The plurality of wives and degradation to which they are subject as widows, which they not unfrequently become while quite children, with the constant state of pupilage in which they are placed,—being while young, under the entire controul of their fathers, when married, under that of their husbands, and when widows, under that of their sons,—or in the absence of them, of their nearest male relative,—perpetuates their degradation to the end of life, and sufficiently accounts for the indifference existing among them with regard to education, to which I have alluded on the preceding page. They may truly be said to endure lives of wretchedness, and to be utterly prostrate as it regards all intellectual and useful knowledge; for sleeping, quarrelling, and puerile conversation are their only recreations; these poor women, our fellow creatures, our fellow immortals, our fellow subjects, are alike destitute of enjoyment here, and of the hope of happiness hereafter!

The low state of moral and religious feeling even among our converts, particularly the grasping covetous disposition which so strongly cleaves to Hindus, and which, alas, has proved a stumbling-block to them as Christians in numerous instances, (though we *have* some bright and happy exceptions,) forms another of our difficulties, and after considering the former it will not create surprise that such should in many instances be the case.

We should guard well against going out with too highly raised expectations in this respect. We cannot justly, and ought not to expect to find in India any general impression of Christianity, and if we do, we shall be sorely disappointed. If we look for a body of converts among the Hindus, equal or superior in attainments, and christian consistency and devotedness, to the members of christian communities in our own land, we are deceiving ourselves, for we can only expect a second and a third generation to begin something like an approximation to those, who have enjoyed for centuries, the privileges and advantages which we have been favoured to possess.

Some of the converts would be an honour to any church, but the majority, even of the truly sincere, are but babes in Christ, or mere children, who are greatly dependent on the training they receive from their spiritual parents. They are teachable, but need line upon line and precept upon precept, and above all a good example in those to whom they naturally look up as their guides and directors. One can well understand when labouring among congregations newly formed from converted heathens, all the exhortations of Paul to Timothy and Titus, with regard to bishops and deacons not being double-tongued, not given to much wine, "to be content with such things as ye have," &c. and his reproofs to the Corinthian and other churches, whom we are apt, perhaps not quite correctly, to look upon as models of perfection. The grossness of their ideas will often discourage us, and shock our sense of propriety, though it may not when we come to analyze it, be so positively sinful as it appears at first. The previous disarrangement of all their moral feelings, the customs and modes of life in which they have grown up, and their old heathen associations, are naturally prone to cleave to them, and those dreadful sins common among heathen, which are not so much as named among us, have, we must remember, been but too familiar with them before they heard the Gospel and were brought under christian influence.* Besides this, the climate of India and the general manners of the Hindus being so dif-

* On one occasion I received a most painful exemplification of this. I was recovering from an illness, and in a very weak state, when one evening a girl from the school came to me and said, S—, naming one of my female servants to whom she knew I was attached, she having been converted in my service, is not so good a woman as you think, she has been angry with us, and has used very bad words. As this girl was addicted to falsehood, I replied, I fear you are bringing a false accusation, which is very naughty. She replied, N— (one of the gardeners) heard her, ask him. I had the man called, and a long

ferent to ours, there are many non-essential points in which they will be likely ever to differ from us, and it sometimes requires discrimination to judge in these matters, for some of our own ideas and usages, though sanctioned by long experience and their own real and intrinsic excellence, are not if we come to examine the matter, found to be absolutely commanded in Scripture, or altogether indispensable to real christian consistency.

investigation took place. He was asked to repeat the expressions, but he said they were so bad, that he could not utter them in my presence. My husband assured him, I should not understand their meaning, but he declared that unless I left the room he could not mention them.

I then went away, and upon their being repeated, the poor accused woman confessed with many tears, that though she was not conscious of it, she admitted the possibility of her having uttered them in her irritation. She added that it grieved her exceedingly, that she had been guilty of such a sin, but as they were from infancy accustomed to hear such expressions, it was extremely difficult for them in unguarded moments to avoid their expression. The whole affair affected my feelings exceedingly—it seemed to me as if a God of *purity* must look upon all this with so much detestation, but yet He bears with these poor weak believers, and must we not learn of Him?

We must be cautious therefore, in expecting more from them than the nature of their circumstances warrant; we must be prepared to exercise patience and forbearance towards them, remembering how much we had ourselves to unlearn and overcome through faith after our own conversion. Thus we shall be enabled, notwithstanding the greatness of the difficulty, cheerfully to persevere in guiding them to such habits, feelings, and ways of acting as are worthy of the Gospel; and if we are so happy as to influence successfully the female part of our converts, we shall considerably lighten the labours of their pastors among them as a whole, for Hindus, though they profess to hold women in such subjection, are actually as much under their influence as others.

I have said rather more on this head than I at first intended, hoping to correct in some measure the many mistakes that exist in the minds of christian females in England (as well as in the church at large) on this particular; and I will now hasten to conclude this letter, only remarking, that though our difficulties and trials are so great and appalling, we must remember, that we are never sent on a warfare at our own charge, and therefore have no need to shrink from encountering them. *We* are but earthen vessels, it is true; but the excellency of the power, both to go forth in his name, and to perform his work, is of God and not of *us*. *He* is far more powerful than all who oppose us, and if we do but wait on Him, He will help us to run without weariness, and to walk without fainting. It is true we may be called to "sow in tears," but it is equally true that we "shall reap in joy," either here or hereafter; for "he that goeth forth weeping bearing precious seed, shall doubtless come again with rejoicing bringing sheaves with him." "He that soweth sparingly" must only expect to reap "sparingly," but "he that soweth bountifully shall reap also bountifully." Sweet and encouraging promises these to the missionary labourer!

Perhaps some may be inclined to think that I exhibit the difficulties connected with our work too strongly, but I can truly say, I only wish to give a fair view of them as they really exist, and to set the light and shade in their true bearings on each other. I have seen persons greatly discouraged at the onset, simply from having come out with too highly raised, and in some measure false and incorrect ideas, and on this account I would guard and caution others. I am convinced, that no one of true genuine missionary principle will be deterred from engaging in the work, because fully led to appreciate the difficulties of it; rather will their ardour be quickened thereby, and their determination to press forward become stronger. "When our hearts are duly set upon the greatest and best objects that can occupy them, we *must* deeply sympathize with the heathen, and shall esteem the sacrifices and labours that may promote their salvation light, for there is placed before us a vocation great beyond the power of language to express, for the privilege of engaging in which, we must deem all oppositions and trifles too small to prevent us."

Yours, &c.

M. W.

LETTER VII.

ON THE KIND OF EFFORTS THAT MAY MOST PROFITABLY BE MADE.

My dear Friend,

It is a matter for thankfulness, that we may now speak of the *variety* of efforts that may be made for the poor degraded females of India. A few years since it seemed almost hopeless to try to make any, but now, blessed be God, an impulse has been given to even this formerly unpromising branch of missionary labour, and our hopes for the final emancipation of the country at large are brightening with the dawn of the long-desired day, when access shall be gained to the hearts and minds of the female population generally.

We must acknowledge that it is as yet but "the day of small things," but we are not on this account to "despise" it, and I am sure none of us feel inclined to do so, but rather to rejoice in it.

The part of our work to be considered first, is that which relates to the care and pains necessary to be taken when placed by the providence of God in connection with a christian congregation. As I have remarked in the previous letter, our native converts in general, and I may here add the females in particular, are but children; and their future consistency and attainments as christian wives and mothers depends very much on the example we set them, and the training they receive from us.

There are different little plans we may pursue according to circumstances, which those very circumstances will suggest, and which can hardly be alluded to on paper; but the chief duties that devolve on us I will try briefly to refer to.

Meetings for prayer among the women I have found to be attended with a very happy effect, for these shew them that we feel a deep interest in their spiritual prosperity, and enable us to direct them to the necessity of prayer, both general and personal, and to recommend and enforce on them the duty and privilege of a regular attendance on public worship, and to impress on them a concern for the salvation of their unconverted relatives and the heathen at large, as well as our own need of the support and encouragement to be derived from their prayers. I think a manifest blessing has been vouchsafed to our little meetings of this sort, both as it respects the christian women, and the unconverted female servants of the house, who are usually willing to attend them.

A meeting for exhortation on Sabbath evenings in a convenient room in the mission house, I have also found to be both attractive and useful. Many of those women whose infants are troublesome in the public services of the morning and afternoon, are glad to avail themselves of this opportunity, and as the instruction given is very simply conveyed, the more ignorant can understand it better than regular discourses.

What the Americans term Maternal Associations, or monthly meetings, for mothers to converse together (with prayer) on the best methods of training their children, and impressing their minds with religious truth, would, I am convinced, be extremely useful; for there is no point on which they more need advice and guidance than this, but as I have not actually tried these, I cannot speak personally as to their effect.

A sort of modified infant school for the younger children is accompanied with a very great and delightful influence, as I have fully proved. We all know that there is not a more direct way to a mother's heart, than that of manifesting an interest in, and a love to, her children. And as example is ever found to possess more power than precept, they are more effectually led to adopt our plans and methods of management from *seeing* their practical workings, and beneficial tendency on their little ones, than from any representations we can make in words. Besides this, it has a number of indirect benefits connected with it, for it leaves them more at liberty to engage in sewing, and other useful employments; and as it respects the children themselves, it has the best effect, for it prepares them, by an efficient early discipline, for becoming much more attentive and teachable pupils when they enter the more advanced schools afterwards. It extends to the young children of both sexes, and we have observed it to have the happiest influence on the mothers, in inducing their own more regular attendance at public worship, to which the habits of little undisciplined children are ever found a great hindrance, even among parents more advanced in every respect than poor Hindu women.

An infant school, therefore, modified in its arrangements, with regard to hours and methods of instruction, according to the different nature of the climate, is, I would say, calculated to be very useful, wherever there is a christian congregation existing. The difficulty of procuring suitable teachers seems one of the greatest obstacles to it, but no doubt that would be overcome by the adoption of some plan for training them, if a great desire were to arise for employing them.

Having tried an infant school, and found it productive of most encouraging results, I can recommend it with particular confidence, as a means of usefulness, which if judiciously *persevered* in, can hardly fail of accomplishing good.

To visit the females in their cottages, and to see to, and insure their comfort in times of trouble and sickness, is such an obvious and natural part of our province, that I need hardly allude to it. In no way can we better gain their confidence and love, than by being near them at these seasons, ready to supply them with such help and medicines as they require, and to apply for their benefit the various simple remedies within our knowledge. A little pains and experience will soon make us mistresses of enough medical skill to be very useful.*

Orphan schools both for boys and girls are now connected with many mission establishments, and have actually realized much good, and promise much more. This is a very plea-

* Perhaps the importance of visiting the women at home, has not always been fully felt, but having practically perceived the great good effected by it, I cannot omit the expression of an earnest hope, that this part of our duty may engage more of our attention and effort generally.

sant and encouragiug branch of labour, the difficulties and trials connected with which, are almost certainly repaid with a greater or more limited degree of success.

When the girls are under our influence for a number of years, *i. e.* from the age of four or five till they are grown up, the former is apparent, and when from circumstances they are not received till their habits and ideas are in a great degree formed, the latter must necessarily be expected. I have on this account been so desirous to get them young, that I have never refused even infants, when I could secure a nurse for them, which their own widowed mothers who brought them to me, were generally willing to become, upon condition of enjoying a sufficient maintenance upon the mission premises, without giving up their caste; which has always been agreed to. In some instances these poor women have voluntarily resigned caste after, and in others they have eventually returned to their villages and friends. Nothing more was required from them than an outward attention to the duties of morality and religion, which they manifested no reluctance to yield, and the private instruction given them, with attendance on public worship, appeared to have in some cases a useful effect.

In these orphan schools the girls are fed and clothed, and brought up in industrious, active, cleanly habits. We have tried to teach them to read well in their own language, and above all to impress their minds with the importance of religion. The daughters of the native Christians have attended daily, if living near enough, and become boarders if at too great a distance. I have found it better, when circumstances permitted it, to unite the mothers with ourselves in the training of their girls, if they were sensible, tractable, industrious women, and have therefore preferred on this, and some other accounts, to have *their* children only as day scholars. It is not possible to train children to domestic habits in a large school, so fully and with so much ease as it can be done by a mother, if she is one who is at all worthy of bearing that name; and besides this, it seems well for parents to be made to remember their personal responsibility, which they are more likely to do, when they find part of their maternal duty devolving on themselves, instead of having it wholly borne by others. I have always aimed likewise to guard against interfering in any of their habits and customs which are harmless, and perhaps better suited for their country and modes of life, than any alterations we could introduce.

To make up for a mother's influence and training in the orphan department, a truly pious and judicious christian couple reside in a cottage appertaining to our orphan school, who both manifest a parental interest in the girls, which is as fully reciprocated by them. The husband is employed in instructing the higher classes, and in conducting the public religious duties of the school, while the wife superintends the cooking and other domestic departments, and looks after the health and comfort of the girls.

These excellent people can approach them in a thousand ways that we cannot, being their own country people, for in every country there exists national peculiarities and feelings with which *natives* only can sympathize together: and as it is seen that they enjoy *our* confidence, that of the children is freely bestowed. I regard such a couple as a necessary auxiliary in a school of this description, without whom it cannot go on perfectly well. European influence and superintendence is always imperfect, and in a degree inefficient, without native co-operation being connected with it.

Besides these, another native couple reside in the school, the wife having herself been brought up among the girls, and being now quite capable of superintending and instructing them, with the assistance of the former, in both the reading and working departments. She is a truly converted character, and exercises a most salutary influence upon the girls in every respect, and being lively, affectionate, and energetic to a degree seldom found among Hindu women, she is not only a general favourite, but an extremely suitable person to aid in forming the characters and habits of the young. *Her* husband is not employed in the school, except in a slight degree in the English department, he having another engagement elsewhere, which occupies the greatest part of his time. Several girls have become pious, and have turned out valuable and useful wives, and in some instances teachers.

This school has also had a very happy effect upon the christian women generally, and has helped to promote a spirit of unity and love, that did not before exist.

Connected with a female orphan and boarding school, we may attempt what I will designate a superior school, *i. e.* a school composed of a smaller number, selected from the orphans, on account of the manifestation of superior abilities, who may be joined by such of the christian girls as are distinguished in a similar way. If this be judiciously managed, it will not excite envy or ill-feeling, at least I have never found it to do so, and while we are so completely shut out from the higher classes as it regards rank, it seems our only alternative for raising up a superior class of women to aid us in future as teachers, and to become suitable wives for the young native Christians of good education, who often marry unsuitably, because they have really no choice. The plan adopted with regard to this superior school is the following.

I have appropriated a suitable room to them in the mission house, the orphan school house being a separate building in the garden, and have endeavoured to bring them up as my own children, with the exception of not altering any of their native customs, with regard to dress, food, bathing in the sun, &c. I have endeavoured carefully to watch their habits, and to instruct them in reading, writing, arithmetic, history, geography, singing, and general knowledge, with all kinds of useful work. After being well able to read in their own language, they learn English, as an additional means of acquiring information, for a Bengalle library does not furnish the necessary books for communicating instruction in some of the above named items. Those among them of a suitable age attend the infant school, and as far as time has allowed the plan to develop, it promises well. I think it very desirable that something of this kind be attempted, of course modified according to circumstances, for the reasons to which I have alluded; and because it gives one a more personal sphere as it were, for we may contrive to impart instruction for a certain time every day, to these girls *ourselves*, without stepping out of our homes, or encountering undue fatigue; and it does strike me that this is one of the most effectual means we at present have, of raising the standard of female character in India, and of improving the very ground-work of society among our native christian *men*. It also seems, as I have had occasion repeatedly to remark, the only prospective plan we can adopt, to prepare suitable and superior instructresses for the better classes, when we begin to gain access to them.

I mention with diffidence another plan, which has been greatly blessed in our orphan school, and mission establishment, yet which may not be considered as generally feasible, although with us it decidedly promotes comfort, as well as usefulness. Certain suitable girls are selected from among the orphans, to become domestic servants in the mission family, one being housemaid, another nursemaid, and so forth. The idea was first suggested by the desire being felt to have only native Christians employed in the house, and the impossibility of getting suitable individuals at the time, as well as from the wish to dispense as far as possible with the services of *men* servants. It not only answers well, but has been found a more effectual means of training these dear girls, both morally and religiously, than the large number congregated in the school permits to be done there, while at the same time they become more active in domestic concerns, and turn out the best wives and mothers of the whole number. It was as a servant in the house, that the natural character of the one now so usefully occupying the post of superintendant in the school was developed, and her heart converted to God; after which she voluntarily requested to be employed in the school, and she has for some years, at first single, and afterwards married, most efficiently filled the situation assigned her there.

One very delightful result arising from the adoption of this plan has been, that ours is, in the strictest sense of the term, a christian establishment, a thing which is not usually found in India. The Sabbath can be observed just as in England, the whole household attending public worship, and the afternoon prayer meeting; and repeating the hymns and portions of Scripture they had learnt during the week evenings, at our usual Sabbath school for the orphans, from twelve till one o'clock. I have never found the plan to interfere in any way with the arrangements necessary to be maintained, or with family order, or with the public engagements of my husband, and I cannot help thinking it might be adopted by others with the same success which has crowned it with us. I quite allow that it involves an additional responsibility on the part of the mistress of the house, and requires her to exercise a constant watchfulness and thoughtfulness; and it needs a certain tact in managing the young domestics, so as to make them willing, obedient, and careful servants; but as we undertake the care of them as orphans, who have no natural parent to bring them up, we may gladly adopt *any* means, that seem most likely to aid us in training these our adopted children *well*, and which will at the same time secure to us their affection and respect, and this I believe we can do, in no way more effectually, than in the one I have alluded to. When the elder ones marry, and new ones have to be selected, there is always so much anxiety manifested to be chosen, as plainly shews the delight and satisfaction the girls themselves feel in being so engaged. Thus I am convinced they become best prepared to watch the cradle of the infant, and to preside in future over the domestic arrangements in their own houses, which so deeply affect the interests of the man.

It seems hardly necessary for me to speak of day schools among heathen natives, as my own experience of them can suggest nothing in their favour. The only children accessible to us, are of the most unpromising class, and their forced attendance, early marriages, and other disadvantages, make it almost a hopeless attempt to try to instruct them at present, with any prospect of reaping fruit in the slightest degree adequate to the time, labour, and expense connected with endeavouring to instruct them. Where however there are a number of Indo-Portuguese children, who are nominal Christians and quite open to christian influence and instruction, a school for them may be a very great means of usefulness.

The Indo-Portuguese are a very degraded people in every respect, and have been a stumbling-block to the heathen, and a hindrance to the missionary in many ways, so that good done to the rising generation among them, is indirectly good done to the natives. I have seen two very flourishing and well conducted day schools for this class of girls under the wives of missionaries, whose situation prevented them from bending their attention to the natives direct. With one of these I am intimately acquainted, and *know* it to have proved hitherto, as it promises to continue to prove, a very marked blessing to the station where it is carried on. The plan pursued in it is attendance from nine till two. The first two hours are occupied in the acquisition of reading, writing, arithmetic, geography, and history, and the last three in useful work. All instruction given, is based upon the Word of God, and as the girls are mostly Roman Catholics this has had a great effect, and the school was primarily, though it may be called indirectly, the means of the conversion of a Roman Catholic Priest, and a respectable and influential family of the same persuasion to the Protestant faith, and what is better to true Christianity. This school is exceedingly well conducted, and contains I believe about forty girls. I should judge such institutions exceedingly promising, for they bid fair to prepare young women, who may hereafter become useful as teachers in infant and other schools, and when it is not possible to procure orphans or christian girls, I would strongly recommend their being tried.

It has also struck me, that those favourably located for it, might endeavour to establish a normal school for training teachers. It must be commenced on a small scale at first, and with the help of competent and devoted superintendants from home for a few years. It would be exceedingly useful if it could be established and efficiently maintained, as well-trained teachers born and brought up in India, would possess many advantages over European ones, and would be obtained with less risk and trouble and at a much smaller cost.

Another means of usefulness, and the last I shall have to suggest, is the preparation of little books, such as are suitable for our female schools, in the native languages, by either translating or compiling them, with the assistance of a good native pundit. This plan has already been tried by one lady, who has presented us with one, and will soon be ready with another valuable little work in Bengalle. I would say that those who have talents for this branch of labour cannot more effectually aid the efforts of missionary females generally, than by occupying themselves in it, for we are cramped in all our labours among women and children, for want of books, and our infant schools, which would be more useful conducted chiefly in Bengalle, have hitherto had to be wholly carried on in English for the same reason. Simple, easy geographies, histories, instructive stories, and little practical works, such as are used in our charity and village schools, are what we at present want.

In some cases it will happen, that from weak health or other inabilities, missionaries' wives will find it impossible to engage in any of the suggested plans, but if they can be real helpmeets to their husbands, encouraging them in their labours, and perhaps corresponding for them, or in some other way saving time to them, they will have no cause to mourn over themselves as utterly unprofitable, though they may ardently long to be more actively engaged.

Perhaps some who could do no more might receive an East Indian or Portuguese female, to wait on them, and attend their children, who manifesting suitable qualifications, might be prepared for a teacher, and eventually given up to any missionary school that might be found needing such a person. I have known two or three instances of useful assistants being supplied in this way.

Yours, &c.

M. W.

LETTER VIII.

A FEW REMARKS UPON THE ENGAGEMENTS ENTERED INTO WITH SINGLE LADIES.

My dear Friend,

I WISH to introduce a few remarks upon the engagement of single females, which strike me as being of importance, before I entirely close.

They chiefly relate to the great care and prudence that should be used, in sending such persons out to India. It is scarcely possible for ladies in England to imagine the difficulties and vexations that may be met by an individual on her arrival, when very definite arrangements have not been completed before she leaves her country, and the parents or relatives who are her natural protectors. I have before observed, and I cannot sufficiently impress the remark upon the minds of all interested in sending out *single* females, that a *young woman* is of all persons, the least calculated, and the least intended to stand *alone.* The character is only fully proved by circumstances, and perhaps few could bear the test, of feeling themselves strangers, in a distant land, with no definite plan of usefulness before them, and no *home* which they can *claim* as their own by right. Persons of very strong mind and firm principles *might* develop better under such circumstances, but it is running by far too great a risk, to subject a female to the test, in a country where every one's circumstances are publicly spoken of and descanted upon. It is true that many would offer to receive a stranger under these circumstances, and missionary families would feel it a duty to protect her, but few, even of the latter, could enter into the peculiarities of her situation, and the zeal of the benevolent and well meaning friends who send her out is thus painfully reflected on, and called into question. Much attention to decorum must be observed on this point, or more harm than good will accrue from the engagement of single ladies,—we must avoid every appearance of evil, and not allow our good to be evil spoken of. We should guard in every possible way, that the minds of the young persons sent out, should have no opportunity of being diverted from the great object for which they go forth, on their arrival in India, for temptations are not wanting, where there is the least opening to allow of their entrance. It strikes me that a set of questions might be addressed to every individual who applies for an assistant similar to the following:

1. What particular department of labour do you propose for our agent in your establishment?

2. What will be the routine of her daily engagements?

3. What time may she consider her own during the day?

4. What facilities will be afforded her for studying the language, and what hours devoted to it?

5. What accommodations will she receive in your house,—and how will she be regarded in your family?

6. What holidays will she enjoy, and at what seasons of the year?

7. What salary will she receive?

8. Do you consider that the sum awarded will be abundantly sufficient to cover her necessary expenses?

9. Do you allow the propriety of our rule, with regard to the term we wish her to continue in our service, and our arrangements regarding her repaying the amount of expense we incur for her, in case of her altering her position with regard to us?

10. Will you permit us to consider you responsible, in union with our agent, for proper arrangements being made in this respect?

11. What provision should you feel it right to make for our agent in case she did not suit you, or you found it advisable on *any* account to dispense with her services?

12. May we *depend* on you for making the necessary arrangements for receiving her on her arrival, and getting her comfortably and safely conveyed to your station, if it should be in the country?

A promise should also be given by the Society in their correspondence with the party,—that in case of the lady proving unfit, from any adequate cause for remaining in India, the party might consider themselves at liberty to send her back at the expense of the Society.*

If these questions were printed with the rules of the Society, in some instances those who applied for a lady could answer them *with* the application, and in others, where this was not done, a delay must be caused of probably six months, to obtain answers to them by an interchange of letters with the party applying. This delay, though it might be inconvenient, would be far better than subsequent disappointment, and it would place the committee, and the party receiving their agent, on a clear understanding together, and would lead the lady also to see exactly how *she* would stand, in her future appointment.

It would be well for all these matters to be clearly stated to her, in the farewell

* I believe a rule of this kind does exist, but it does not seem in all instances to have been understood. As the rules are not perhaps read with sufficient attention, a distinct reference to this particular in the preliminary correspondence is desirable.

letters of instructions which I believe it is customary to give.

Very definite and complete answers should, I think, be required to such a set of enquiries, on the plea, that the ladies feel themselves responsible for the future comfort and usefulness of their agents, and deem it necessary to have an assurance in *writing*, of all these matters before-hand, though they give full credit to the party applying, for every disposition to kindness and consideration. Too much should never be taken for granted,—in affairs that ought to be regarded as matters of business,—even from missionaries, though we can readily believe that every one applying for an assistant would be prepared to treat her with kindness, to regard her as a sister, and to aim to make her as comfortable as possible.

If it be thought that offence would be taken at these enquiries, and that the parties applying would decline, or be discouraged from receiving a lady in consequence, such parties would certainly be better without the charge, but I believe *this* would scarcely occur.

If but a very small number of well qualified ladies be sent out, on sure and certain promises of protection and support, more real good will be done, and greater encouragement gained, than by sending out a larger number less advantageously located.

I have heard it suggested, that only as many agents be sent as the Society can themselves support, but as the chief thing unmarried females require in India is *protection*, I believe the other plan would be preferable.

Yours, &c.
M. W.

APPENDIX.

RULES WITH REGARD TO HEALTH.

1. OBSERVE habitual temperance in eating and drinking, beginning to do so, as soon as you commence the voyage from England. This is of the first importance, and under God's blessing, I do believe that if prudence be observed in this, a great deal of failure of health from change of climate may be avoided. We must remember that we are exotics in India, and cannot use those freedoms we do in our native country. We should carefully ascertain what diet seems to suit our constitution best, and resolutely abstain from every thing, however agreeable to our palate, that appears to do us harm. Some of our best missionaries attribute a good degree of the health they have enjoyed to care in this respect, and regularity in the times of our meals is of as much importance as temperance. The temp-

tation to drink quantities of water and acids is great, from the thirst produced by constant perspiration, but the evil is only increased by gratification, and the less one can drink between meals the better, and the less, when accustomed to it, is suffered from thirst. No rules can be given as to articles of diet, as different persons are differently affected. We must eat and drink what may best suit ourselves individually, and perhaps it will be found to be quite contrary to what agreed best with us in Europe.

2. Bathe every morning, *if* it agree with you, and ascertain whether cold or tepid water suit you best. Some people cannot bathe frequently, and others feel refreshed by doing so. Water slightly tepid generally agrees best in Bengal. The head should be washed, as a general rule, as often as one bathes.

3. Endeavour to be in bed by ten. To retire early is of much more importance in India than in Europe. I never knew persons, except one or two of extraordinary constitutions, who did not eventually repent inattention to this rule. Rise as early as you like, and if possible, take a good walk *before*, or immediately after sun-

rise. This is one of the greatest preservatives of health, and better for many persons than horse exercise.

4. Rest for an hour when you feel tired, which will generally be about two or three. It is no loss of time to take an hour's repose, as it fits you to labour after.

5. Avail yourself of the benefit of a punkah, if you find it save your strength. It is a great blessing to have any means at command by which you may alleviate the effects of the dreadful heat; and it is a mistake to call it an indulgence, if it prevent you from becoming unduly exhausted; but one must avoid being a slave to it.

6. Avoid exposure to the sun, especially till you are in some degree acclimated. No European can appreciate the danger of this, till taught it by experience. You must yield to the advice of those who have resided in India. Many valuable lives have been sacrificed to not heeding cautions on this head.

7. Endeavour to maintain habitual cheerfulness. "A merry heart doeth good like a medicine," for the mind influences the health amazingly in a tropical climate.

8. Relax from five or six in the evening for at least two hours, and take a walk, or if you have opportunity, a drive. You may then feel equal to employ yourself again in the evening till nine.

To sum up all in a few words; a simple and light diet, a tranquil mind, caution against sudden changes in the air, and moderate exercise, seem to be the most necessary things to preserve health in Bengal. All extremes are to be avoided, and regular habits to be cultivated in every respect.

FINIS.

HAND BOOK
OF
SINHALESE GRAMMAR

WITH EXERCISES

ON OLLENDORFF'S SYSTEM

HAND BOOK
OF
SINHALESE GRAMMAR

WITH EXERCISES

ON OLLENDORFF'S SYSTEM

SIMON DE SILVA

GYAN

Published by

Gyan Publishing House
5, Ansari Road
Daryaganj, New Delhi-110002
Phone: 011-47034999, 9811692060
E-mail: books@gyanbooks.com

Distribution Network
gyanbooks.com
India, USA, Canada, UK, Australia, France

ISBN : 978-81-212-4417-6 (PB)
First Published, Colombo, 1922

2nd Impression 2020

Printed at: Gyan Press, Delhi.

The book at your disposal is the edition of an old book originally published long back. The Text quality of this book may not be at par as compared to our other books but many readers approached us to reprint this important book so that it could satiate their hunger. We request all the readers of this book to help us to improve its quality by providing the necessary text of those pages which are not properly visible. Your valuable support in this case will be highly appreciated and acknowledged and our future readers will be benefitted immensely.

HAND BOOK

OF

SINHALESE GRAMMAR

WITH EXERCISES

ON OLLENDORFF'S SYSTEM

BY

SIMON DE SILVA

Mudaliyar of the Governor's Gate

and

Chief Sinhalese Translator to Ceylon Government.

PRINTED BY

J. D. FERNANDO AT THE GRANTHAPRAKAKA PRESS COLOMBO.

1922

PREFACE.

THE main aim of this little book is to help Europeans to acquire a knowledge of colloquial Sinhalese. Experience as a Pandit has convinced the author of the necessity of a work on these lines; and it will be found that he has paid special attention to those questions which usually puzzle the foreigner. For the exercises he has carefully selected such expressions as are frequently used by the officers of the Government in their communications with minor headmen.

INDEX.

APPENDIX.

ERRATA.

PAGE.

2 Linc 15 Delete "," after the word " the. "

3 „ 6 the second " ඵ " should be " ඵෑ. "

9 Para I7 In the second line read " Substituting " for " Substuting. "

10 Para 18 1st line read " combination " for "comination."

17 Para 31 In the last line the last word should be " perceive. "

17 Para 32 In the second line " intial " should be " initial. "

28 Para 59 In Examples after the root letter සා fill in blank with " to plough. "

30 Line 4 Read " to cook " for " to Coock. "

30 Line 20 Read " මැරැවා " for " මරැවා . "

46 In Exercise Line 6 Read " පියාඹනවා " for " පියාබ නවා. "

47 Page 94 Ist line Read " Infinitive " for " infanative. "

60 Line 4 Read " buried " for " burricd. "

61 Para 115 2nd line Read " කිලුපුල් " for " කිලුප්ල්. "

73 In Vocabulary 10 thè first word should be " ඇතුල් කරනවා. "

74 In the last line the second word should be " fight. "

1C0 The meaning of the word " සම්පූර්ණ " should be read as " pcrfect. "

101 The meaning of the word හැඟෙනවා " should be read as " to perceive. "

1C6 Read " meet " for " met. "

111 The word following " tod-ay " should be " to-morrow "

111 The word following " true " is " truth. "

112 Read " Waste lands " for " Wast lands. "

SINHALESE GRAMMAR

— AND —

EXERCISES.

INTRODUCTION.

THE SINHALESE ALPHABET.

VOWELS. පණකුරු.

අ a ආ à; ඇ ẹ, ඈ ẹ́; ඉ i, ඊ í; උ u, ඌ ú; ඍ ṛi ඎ ṛí;
ඏ lṛi, ඐ lṛí; එ e, ඒ é, ඓ ai; ඔ o, ඕ ó, ඖ au;
ං (anuswàra) ṇ, ඃ (visarga) h.

CONSONANTS. ගතකුරු

Gutturals ක ka, ඛ kha, ග ga, ඝ gha, ඞ na,
Palatals ච cha, ඡ chha, ජ ja, ඣ jha, ඤ ña,
Cerebrals ට ṭa, ඨ ṭha, ඩ ḍa, ඪ ḍha, ණ ṇa,
Dentals ත ta, ථ tha, ද da, ධ dha, න na,
Labials ප pa, ඵ pha, බ ba, භ bha, ම ma,
Semi-vowels ය ya, ර ra, ල la, ළ ḷa, ව wa or va,
Sibilants ශ ṣa, ෂ sha, ස sa,
Aspirate හ h.

The vowels should be pronounced as follows :—viz.

අ like the first **a** in mamma.
ආ like **a** in father.
ඇ like **a** in cat.
ඈ like **a** in bank.
ඉ like **i** in it.
ඊ like **i** in police.
උ like **u** in full.
ඌ like **u** in rule
එ like the first **e** in there
ඒ like **a** in able.
ඓ like **ai** in aisle.
ඔ like **o** in opinion.
ඕ like **o** in go.
ඖ like **ow** in cow.

The Consonants are, in general, pronounced as in English.

The above forms of the vowels are used only at the beginning of a syllable The vowel අ is inherent in every consonant, and is sounded after every one which has not the mark ් or ් shewing that it is deprived of vowel sound

The other vowels, when not used at the beginning of a syllable, are represented by the following symbols:—

ආ=ා, ඇ=ැ, ඈ=ෑ ඉ= ි, ඊ= ී, උ= ු or ැ, ඌ= ූ or ෑ, ඍ=ෘ, ඎ=ෲ, ඏ=ෟ, ඐ=ෳ. එ=ෙ, ඒ=ෙ—්, ඓ=ෛ ඔ=ෙ—ා, ඕ=ෙ—ෝ, ඖ=ෙ—ෟ.

A consonant, deprived of vowel sound, bears, as already stated, the mark ් or ්, thus:—ම්, ක්. The former mark is appended to letters ending in a line turned upwards, as ව, ම, බ &c.; and the latter to all the rest.

Examples of the combination of vowel symbols with the, consonants ක් and ම්

ක් + අ	=	ක	ම් + අ	=	ම
ක් + ආ	=	කා	ම් + ආ	=	මා
ක් + ඇ	=	කැ	ම් + ඇ	=	මැ
ක් + ඈ	=	කෑ	ම් + ඈ	=	මෑ
ක් + ඉ	=	කි	ම් + ඉ	=	මි
ක් + ඊ	=	කී	ම් + ඊ	=	මී
ක් + උ	=	කු	ම් + උ	=	මු
ක් + ඌ	=	කූ	ම් + ඌ	=	මූ
ක් + ඍ	=	කෘ	ම් + ඍ	=	මෘ
ක් + ඎ	=	කෲ	ම් + ඎ	=	මෲ
ක් + ඏ	=	කෟ	ම් + ඏ	=	මෟ
ක් + ඐ	=	කෳ	ම් + ඐ	=	මෳ
ක් + එ	=	කෙ	ම් + එ	=	මෙ
ක් + ඒ	=	කේ	ම් + ඒ	=	මේ
ක් + ඓ	=	කෛ	ම් + ඓ	=	මෛ
ක් + ඔ	=	කො	ම් + ඔ	=	මො
ක් + ඕ	=	කෝ	ම් + ඕ	=	මෝ
ක් + ඖ	=	කෞ	ම් + ඖ	=	මෞ

Of the symbols of ු and ූ, ු and ූ are appended to the letters ක, ග, ඤ, ත, භ, ර, ශ, thus:—කු, කූ, ගු, ගූ, ඤු, ඤූ, තු, තූ, භු, භූ, රු, රූ, ශු, ශූ; and ු and ූ to the rest of the letters, thus:—බු, බූ, ළු, ළූ, &c.

The letter ළ, when combined with ු and ූ takes the forms of ළු and ළූ respectively.

The latter ර්, when it immediately precedes a vowelconsonant,* is written above it in the form of ◌ර්, thus:—ර්ග rga; and when ර immediately follows a mute consonant is written as a slanting line beneath it, thus:—ග්‍ර gra.

The letter ය following a mute consonant is written ්‍ය, thus:—ක්‍ය kya, ස්‍ය sya.

When two consonants meet without the intervention of a vowel, they coalesce and become one conjunct letter. The following are the most frequently recurring.

Conjunct Letters. බැඳිඅකුරු.

ක්ව kva,	ක්ෂ ksha,	ඥ jña,	ට්ඨ ttha,	ත්ථ ttha,
ත්ව tva,	ද්ධ ddha,	ද්ව dwa,	ක්‍ය kya,	ක්‍ර kra,
ර්ම rma,	ඟ nga,	ඤ්ච nhca,	ඦ nja,	ඬ nda,
න්ථ ntha,	ඳ nda,	න්ධ ndha,	ඹ mba,	

The conjunct letters ඟ, ඬ, ඳ, ඹ, in pure Sinhalese, are coalitions of a semi-nasal with ග, ඩ, ද, බ.

---

* A vowel-consonant is a consonant with a vowel incorporated, as ක, කා, කි &c.,

LESSON I. 1 පාඩම

1. A Sinhalese noun as it stands in the Dictionary is in the form used as Nominativ Singular.

2 A masculine noun generally ends in ආ, as in මිනිහා man; a feminine in අ, ඊ, ඉනි &c., as in බිසව queen, ඌරි sow, යකිනි she-devil; and a neuter or inanimate noun in අ or එ, as in අත hand, කුඩේ umbrella.

Stems of Nouns. නාමප්‍රකෘති.

3. The stem of a noun may be obtained from the form in which it stands for the nominative singular by elision or substitution of letters, according to the following rules.

Animate Nouns.

1. If a noun ends in කා, තා, නා, ලා, or සා (හා), not preceded by උ or ඌ or a mute consonant of the same kind, the stem may be obtained by eliding the final ආ.

EXAMPLES. උදාහරණ

Nom: Singular	Stem
හරකා ox	හරක්
ඇතා elephant	ඇත්
ගොනා bull	ගොන්
හිවලා jackal	හිවල්
මිනිහා (මිනිසා) man	මිනිස්

5. If a noun ends in ටා, ඩා ණා, දා, රා, or ළා, not preceded by උ, ඌ, or a mute consonant, the stem may be obtained by substituting අ for the final ආ.

EXAMPLES උදාහරණ.

Nom: Singular	Stem
කොටා short man	කොට
ලෙඩා patient	ලෙඩ
කණා blind man	කණ
වෙදා medical man	වෙද
හොරා thief	හොර
දෙමළා Tamil	දෙමළ

6. If in a noun the final vowel-consonant is preceded by උ or ඌ, the stem may be obtained by substituting උ for the final vowel ආ.

EXAMPLES. උදාහරණ.

Nom: Singular	Stem
ඌරා pig	ඌරු
කුකුළා cock	කුකුළු
බමුණා Brahman	බමුණු
කපුටා crow	කපුටු
වවුලා bat	වවුලු
හුණා lizard	හුණු

7. If the final vowel-consonant is preceded by a mute consonant of the same kind, the stem is obtained by eliding the final vowel-consonant and adding ඉ or උ to the preceding mute consonant.

Note :—If the vowel before the mute consonant is අ, උ, or ඔ, the vowel උ is added to the mute consonant; if ඇ, ඉ or එ, the vowel ඉ is added.

EXAMPLES. උදාහරණ.

Nom: Singular	Stem.
බල්ලා dog	බලු
කුරුල්ලා bird	කුරුලු
කොල්ලා lad	කොලු
වැද්දා hunter	වැදි
ඉබ්බා tortoise	ඉබි
බෙල්ලා oyster	බෙලි

8. If a noun ends in යා or වා (ය් or ව් being an * augmentation) not preceded by අ, the stem may be obtained by eliding යා or වා as the case may be.

---

* Augmentation is a letter inserted between the root and the suffix.

EXAMPLES උදාහරණ.

Nom: Singular	Stem
දිවියා leopard	දිවි
වඩුවා carpenter	වඩු.

Note:—In words like නයා cobra, මුවා deer, the letters යා and වා being radicals should not be elided. Their stems are respectively නයි and මුව.

9 If a noun ends in යා or වා (ය් or ව් being an augmentation) preceded by a consonant with the inherent vowel අ, the stem may be obtained by eliding යා or වා and lengthening the preceding අ.

EXAMPLES උදාහරණ

Nom: Singular	Stem
ළමයා boy	ළමා
ගිරවා parrot	ගිරා
රදවා washer man	රදා

EXERCISE 1. 1 අභ්‍යාස පාඩම

Write down the stem of each of the following words.

Vocabulary 1.

මකුණා	bug	වලහා (වලසා)	bear
කොකා	crane	වස්සා	calf
අශ්වයා	horse	වඳුරා	ape
බූරුවා	ass	රිළවා	monkey
යහළුවා	friend	මැස්සා	fly
මීයා	rat	සතුරා	enemy
තිරිසනා	brute	ගොළුවා	dumb man
බළලා	cat	කොටියා	cheetah
වස්සා	calf	මිතුරා	friend
බැටළුවා	sheep	කොරා	lame man
දාසයා	slave	කැරපියා	cockroach
ළදරුවා	infant	අලියා	elephant

LESSON II. 2 පාඩම.

Inanimate Nouns. අප්‍රාණිශබ්ද.

10. If a noun ends in ක, ත, න, ප, බ, ම, ල, or ස, the stem may generally be obtained by eliding the inherent vowel අ.

EXAMPLES. උදාහරණ.

Nom: Singular	Stem
මැණික gem	මැණික්
අත hand	අත්
කන ear	කන්
ලිප hearth	ලිප්
ගැබ womb	ගැබ්
ගම village	ගම්
මල flower	මල්
ගහ (ගස) tree	ගස්

11. In nouns ending in ට, ඩ, ණ, ද, ර, ළ, not preceded by උ or ඌ, the stem is the same as the nominative singular; but, if preceded by උ or ඌ, the final අ is changed into උ, and if preceded by ඉ, the final අ is changed into ඉ.

EXAMPLES. උදාහරණ

Nom: Singular	Stem	Nom: Singular	Stem
කට mouth	කට	සතුට pleasure	සතුටු
බඩ belly	බඩ	තුඩ beak	තුඩු
අණ command	අණ	ලකුණ sign	ලකුණු
පොද drop	පොද	මුහුද sea	මුහුදු
පාර road	පාර	හුළ torch	හුළු
වළ pit	වළ	ඉර line	ඉරි
		මිට fist	මිටි

Exception:—The stem of කද pingo is කඳ්

12. If the final vowel–consonant of a noun is preceded by a mute consonant of the same kind the stem may be obtained by eliding the final vowel consonant and appending ඉ or උ to the preceding mute consonant, as in masculine nouns. See note to rule 7.

EXAMPLES. උදාහරණ.

Nom: Singular		Stem
ඉත්ත	twig	ඉති
පොල්ල	club	පොලු

13. If a noun ends in ය or ව (ය් or ව් being an augmentation) the stem may be obtained by eliding ය or ව.

EXAMPLFS. උදාහරණ

Nom: Singular		Stem
අඩිය	foot	අඩි
පුටුව	chair	පුටු

14. If a noun ends in ඒ, the stem may be obtained by substituting ඇ for ඒ.

EXAMPLES. උදාහරණ.

Nom: Singular		Stem
කඩේ	boutique	කඩ
කුඩේ	umbrella	කුඩ

Exception:—The stem of කිරේ (arecanut cutter) is කිරා.

15. In names of things, which are weighed or measured, the stem is th same as the nominative

EXAMPLES. උදාහරණ.

Nom: Singular		Stem
පැණි	honey	පැණි
සීනි	sugar	සීනි
කිරි	milk	කිරි

16. If a noun ends in ඟ or ඳ (conjunct letters), the stem may be obtained by eliding the consonant ඟ or ඳ and substituting a full nasal for the semi-nasal.

EXAMPLES. උදාහරණ.

Nom Singular		Stem
අඟ	horn	අං
ගඟ	river	ගං
මඟ	vay	මං
හුළඟ	wind	හුළං
ළිඳ	well	ළින්
වළඳ	pan	වළන්
කළඳ	drachm	කළන්

Exceptions :—

ඇඳ	bed	ඇඳ
කඳ	trunk of a tree, body	කඳ
හඳ	moon	හඳ
ඇඟ	body	ඇඟ

Note:—ඟ is a coalition of semi ං and ග්, and ඳ of semi න් and ද

17. If a noun ends in න්ද, the stem may be obtained by substuting the semi nasal for the full nasal and ඉ or උ for the final අ. See note to Rule 7.

EXAMPLFS. උදාහරණ

Nom: Singular		Stem
හැන්ද	spoon	හැඳි
කන්ද	mountain	කඳු

EXERCISE II. 2 අභ්‍යාස පාඩම.

Write down the stems of the following words.

Vocabulary 2.

ගල	stone	නියර	ridge
නූල	thread	අගල	ditch
වැට	fence	ගෙදර	home

අත්ත branch
යතුර key
මුල root
වත්ත garden
ඉත්ත fence stick
වැව tank
හාල් rice
පාලම bridge
කෙන්ද fibre
කඩදාසිය paper
පොකුණ pond
ගෙය house
පොත book
පෙට්ටිය box
ලියුම letter
වෙල field
බෙල්ල neck
යකඩ iron

LESSON III. 3 පාඩම.

3. Combination. සන්ධි.

18. Sandhi is the comination of two words or of a word and a syllable.

19. In such combination some change of letters takes place According to the nature of this change, Sandhi is divided into ten classes, viz

(1.) පෙරසරලොප්සඳ or පූර්වස්වරලෝපසන්ධි.

(1.) Combination by the elision of the preceding vowel.

This combination is effected by the elision of the final vowel of the first word.

EXAMPLES. උදාහරණ.

නුවණ + ඇති = නුවණැති having wisdom
දින + ඉසුරු = දිනිසුරු sun.
හිඟුරු + අල = හිඟුරල a kind of yam.

(2) පරසරලොප්සඳ or පරස්වරලෝපසන්ධි.

(2.) Combination by the elision of the following vowel.

In this combination the intial vowel of the second word is elided.

EXAMPLES. උදාහරණ.

රජ + උතුමා = රජතුමා great king
පණ + අකුරු = පණකුරු vowels.

(3) සරසඳ or ස්වරසන්ධි.

(3) Vowel combination.

In this combination there is no elision but the intial vowel of the second word coalesce with the final mute consonant of the first word.

EXAMPLES. උදාහරණ.

මිනිස් + එක් = මිනිසෙක් a man.
එකින් + එක = එකිනෙක one by one

(4) සරදෙස්සඳ or ස්වරාදේශ සන්ධි.

(4.) Combination by substitution of Vowls.

This combination is effected by the substution of one vowel in the place of two vowels. The vowels that are generally substituaed are එ or ඒ for අ and ඉ; ඔ or ඕ for අ and උ.

EXAMPLES. උදාහරණ.

මහ + ඉසුරු = මෙහෙසුරු
මහ + උර = මොහොර

(5) ගතදෙස් සඳ or ගාත්‍රාදේශසන්ධි.

(5) Cambination by the Substitution of Consonants.

EXAMPLES. උදාහරණ

දඬු + කම් = දඬුවම් punishment.
පිළි + කම් = පිළියම් remedy.

(6) පෙරරු සඳ or පූර්වරූප සන්ධි.

(6.) Assimilation of the following letter to the preceding consonant.

ගෙත් + කම් = ගෙත්තම් weaving.
කම් + හල් = කම්මල් smith's forge.

(7) පරරූ සඳ or පරරූපසන්ධි

(7.) Assimilation of the preceding consonant to the following letter.

EXAMPLES. උදාහරණ.

දුක් + පත් = දුප්පත් poor.
අත් + ලස් = අල්ලස් bribe.

(8) ගතකුරුලොප්සඳ or ගාත්‍රාක්ෂරලෝප සන්ධි.

(8.) Combination by the elision of consonants.

In this combination the final vowel–consonant of the first word is elided and the semi–nasal before it is augmented.

EXAMPLES. උදාහරණ.

කොළඹ + පුර = කොළොම්පුර Colombo.
ගඟ + ඉවුර= ගංඉවුර river bank.

(9) අගම් සඳ or ආගමසන්ධි.

(9.) Combination by the insertion of a consonant.

EXAMPLES. උදාහරණ.

පුන + උත් = පුනුරුත් tautology.
දිවි + ආ = දිවියා leopard.

(10) දෙරූ සඳ or ද්විරූපසන්ධි.

(10.) Combination by reduplication of the consonant.

EXAMPLES. උදාහරණ.

හෙළිලි + අ ඹු= හෙළිල්ලඹු.
කුළු + එව් — කුල්ලෙව්.

EXERCISE III. 3 අභ්‍යාස පාඩම.

(*a*) Combine the following pairs of words according to the rules of සන්ධි.

එකින් + එක; කවු + අ; ගත + අකුරු;
ගන + එන; නිල් + උපුල්; මැති + උතුමා;

කටු + අල; පස් + ඇස්; මිනිස් + හු;
උක් ÷ ගස් නිල් + උපුල් කොළු + ආ;
ගඟ + තෙර; සුරු + අත; පුත් + හු;
උඩ + අල; අ + අදර; සහ + උදර
වම් + අත; වම් + ඇස; සුර + අඟන.

(*b*) Resolve the following compounds into their component parts

සිත්තරු; ලිග්ගල්; නිරවුල්; පඬිතුමා,
වියවුල්; පසැස්; ගෙනෙන; කටුවල;
නරනිඳු; බතල; සත්තු; දිනිඳු;
වමැස සිවුරඟ; ගංවතුර; උග්ගස්;
සිංහයා; වඩුවා; කුරුල්ලා; වැද්දා;
පිනැති; ගොක්කොළ; බතල; නිරවුල්;
මහොත්තම; හිතොපදෙශ, නරෙන්ද්‍ර; මැතිඳු.

LESSON IV. 4 පාඩම.

4. Gender. ලිඞ්ග or ලිඟු.

20 There are three genders in Sinhalese viz., පුංලිඞ්ග masculine gender, ස්ත්‍රීලිඞ්ග feminine gender and නපුංසක ලිඞ්ග neuter gender.

21. Masculine is generally expressed by adding ආ and feminine by adding ඊ, ඉනී, ඉන්න &c., to the stem, which is common to both the genders.

Examples. උදාහරණ.

Stem	Masculine		Feminine
ඇත්	ඇතා	elephant	ඇතිනි, ඇතින්න
ඌරු	ඌරා	pig	ඊරි
කපුටු	කපුටා	crow	කපුටි
කුකුළු	කුකුළා	cock	කිකිළි
කුරුලු	කුරුල්ලා	bird	කිරිල්ලි
කොක්	කොකා	crane	කෙකී
ගිරා	ගිරවා	parrot	ගිරවි

තරුණ	තරුණයා youngman	තරුණී
නාග	නාගයා cobra	නැගිනී
පිස්සු	පිස්සා mad man	පිස්සි
බළල්	බළලා cat	බැළලී
බලු	බල්ලා dog	බැල්ලී
මුනුබුරු	මුනුබුරා grandson	මිනිබිරි
යහළු	යහළුවා friend	යෙහෙළි
යක්	යකා devil	යකිනී, යකින්න
වලස්	වලහා (වලසා) bear	වැලහිනී
හරක්	හරකා ox	හරකී

22. The feminine of some words are formed from the masculine by change of vowels.

EXAMPLES. උදාහරණ

Mas :	Fem :
මේ this (man)	මෝ this (woman)
මූ this one	මෑ this one
ඌ he	ඈ she
තෝ you	තී you
කොරා lame man	කෙර lame woman.
මහල්ලා old man	මැහැල්ල old woman
හොරා thief (man	හෙර thief (woman)
කොල්ලා lad	කෙල්ල lass

23. The feminine of some words is expressed by joining to the stem another word denoting feminine.

EXAMPLES උදාහරණ.

Stem.	Masculine.	Feminine.
එළු	එළුවා goat	එළුදෙන්
මුව	මුවා deer	මුවදෙන්
මෘග	මෘගයා beast	මෘගදෙනුව
සිංහ	සිංහයා lion	සිංහදෙනුව

24. In the case of the name of some living beings the masculine and feminine are denoted by different words.

EXAMPLES. උදාහරණ.

Masculine.	Feminine.
මාමා maternal uncle, father in law	නැන්දා aunt, mother in law
අප්පා father	අම්මා mother
අය්යා elder brother	අක්කා elder sister
අශ්වයා horse	වෙළඹ, ලෙම්බ mare
ඉලන්දාරියා young man	ලමිස්සි young woman
ගොනා bull	දෙන් cow
පියා father	මව් mother
පුතා son	දූ daughter
පුරුෂයා man, husband	ස්ත්‍රී woman, wife
බෑනා nephew, son in law	ලේලී niece, daughter in law
මලයා younger brother	නගා, නංගී, younger sister
මස්සිනා brother in law	නෑනා sister in law
මිනිහා man	ගෑනී woman
රජ king	බිසව queen
සීයා grand father	ආච්චි grandmother

EXERCISE IV. 4 අභ්‍යාස පාඩම.

(*a*) Give the Feminine forms of the following masculine nouns.

කුකුළා, බළලා, යහළුවා, මුනුබුරා, නයා
කොරා, කොල්ලා, මලයා, මාමා, බෑනා
ගොනා, සිංහයා, ඌ අශ්වයා සීයා
මස්සිනා, එළුවා, හොරා, මූ, තෝ,
රජ, මිනිහා, මේ පියා, මහල්ලා,

(*b*) Give the masculine and feminine forms of the following noun stems

කොක්, කුමර, දෘශ, රකුසු, වසු, රිළා
යක්, සතුරු, සුදු, මොනර, යෝධ, වැදි,
බමුණු, බළල්, වලස්, ගිරු, කුකුළු, කුරුලු,
මිනිස්, ගොන්, මහලු, පුරුෂ වඳුරු එළු

LESSON V. 5 පාඩම.

5. ARTICLES.

25. There are no equivalents in Sinhalese of the articles **a** or **an** and **the**

26. The idea of the indefinite is expressed by suffixing එක් or අක් to the stem, as මිනිස් + එක් = මිනිසෙක් a man : ගෑනි + අක් = ගෑනියක් a woman : ගල් + අක් = ගලක් a stone.

Note:—එක් is suffixed to masculine and අක් to feminine and neuter nouns

Note:—Suffixes are added to stems according to the rules of සන්ධි.

EXERCISE V. 5 අභ්‍යාසපාඩම.

Write down, in English, the meaning of the following, taking the words from Vocabularies 1 and 2.

අශ්වයෙක්, යාළුවෙක්, ගලක්, සතුරා, වැටක්, අශ්වයා, අත් තක්, පාලමක්, කඩදාසියක්, මීයෙක්, බළලා, කොකෙක්, මැස් සෙක්, ගෙයක්, වත්තක්, යතුරක්, ගෙදර, අගලක්, නියර, වැවක්.

Write down in Sinhalese, the meaning of the following. A stone, a letter, a rat, the ridge, an enemy, an ape, a fence stick the monkey, an ass, the dumb man, a root, the house, a book, the thread, a fly, a crane the bear, a tank.

LESSON VI. 6 පාඩම.

6. VERBS. ක්‍රියා

27. A Sinhalese verb as it stands in the Dictionary is in the form colloquially used as present tense indicative irrespective of person and number as කපනවා cut, දුවනවා run, පෙනෙනවා appear.

28. The root of a verb is obtained by eliding the termination නවා.

29. The verbs, of which the final vowel of the root is අ or ඉ, are generally volitive, as මරනවා kill අදිනවා drag.

30. The verbs, of which the vowel before the tense-affix is එ, are involitive (නිරුත්සාහක ක්‍රියා), as වැටෙනවා fall, පෙනෙනවා appear.

31. An involitive verb expresses an act done without the effort or the will of the doer.

EXAMPLES. උදාහරණ.

වැවෙනවා grow, පැසෙනවා ripen, පාවෙනවා float, දිලිසෙනවා shine වෙනවා become, ළංවෙනවා approach, මැරෙනවා die, සිනාසෙනවා laugh, ඇහෙනවා hear, දැනෙනවා feel, හැඟෙනවා percieve.

32. Volitive verbs may be made involitive by changing the final vowel of the root into එ and the intial vowels as follows:

අ	into	ඇ
ආ	„	ඈ
උ	„	ඉ
ඌ	„	ඊ
ඔ	„	එ
ඕ	„	ඒ

The initial vowels ඉ and එ remain unchanged.

EXAMPLES. උදාහරණ.

Volitive		Involitive
කපනවා	cut	කැපෙනවා
සාදනවා	make	සෑදෙනවා
දුවනවා	run	දිවෙනවා
සූරනවා	scrape	සීරෙනවා
ඔතනවා	wrap round	එතෙනවා
සෝදනවා	wash	සේදෙනවා
ඉරනවා	tear	ඉරෙනවා
පෙරළනවා	overturn	පෙරළෙනවා

33. Where the root is a monosyllable the එ coalesces with ව.

EXAMPLFS. උදාහරණ.

Volitive		Involitive
කනවා	eat	කැවෙනවා
දෙනවා	give	දෙවෙනවා
හානවා	plough	හැවෙනවා
බොනවා	drink	පෙවෙනවා

EXERCISE VI. 6. අභ්‍යාස පාඩම.

Vocabulary 3.

(*a*) Change the following volitive verbs into involitive.

කරනවා	do	හාරනවා	dig	යනවා	go
අල්ලනවා	catch	කඩනවා	break	බඳිනවා	bind
පියාඹනවා	fly	අදිනවා	drag	අරිනවා	open, send
විකුණනවා	sell	පනිනවා	jump	පීනනවා	swim
ඇවිදිනවා	walk	බුරනවා	bark	එනවා	come
නානවා	bathe	වවනවා	grow	වදිනවා	rush in
ලියනවා	write	කියවනවා	read	කියනවා	say
නගිනවා	ascend	බහිනවා	descend	අඬනවා	cry
මනිනවා	measure	ගිලිනවා	swallow	නැගිටිනවා	rise up
සිඹිනවා	kiss	ගන්නවා	take	ගහනවා	beat
වපුරනවා	sow	මහනවා	sew	පදිනවා	row
බනිනවා	abuse	නටනවා	dance	සෙල්ලම්කරනවා	play

(*b*) Write down, in English, the meaning of the following phrases.

කොකා පියාඹනවා. ගල කැඩෙනවා. මීයා පනිනවා. යහළුවා ඇවිදිනවා. ඉත්ත කැඩෙනවා. හාල් විකිණෙනවා. මූල කැපෙනවා. පෙට්ටිය ඇරෙනවා. මිනිහා නානවා. පොත ඉරෙනවා. ගෙය සෑදෙනවා. වත්ත වැවෙනවා. වැව හැරෙනවා. අශ්වයා දුවනවා බළලා අල්ලනවා. ඔරුව පැදෙනවා. වඩුවා කපනවා. ළමයා කියවනවා. රදවා සෝදනවා. දිවියා දුවනවා. ගිරවා කනවා.

LESSON VII. 7 පාඩම.

7. FORMATION OF THE PLURAL. බහුවචන සෑදීම.

Animate Nouns. ප්‍රාණවාචක ශබ්ද.

34. The plural of animate nouns is generally formed by adding ඕ, නු or උ to the stem.

35. If the stem ends in ඉ or උ, the plural is generally formed by adding ඕ.

36. If the stem ends in a mute consonant, the plural is formed by adding නු.

37 If the stem ends in අ in coalition with ර, the plural is formed by adding උ.

Note 1:—The plural termination නු is generally assimilated to the preceding consonant.

Note 2:—Case terminations are suffixed to the stems of words in accordance with the rules of Sandhi (සන්ධි).

EXAMPLES. උදාහරණ.

Stem	Singular		Plural
වැදි	වැද්දා hunter		වැද්දෝ (දෙරුසඳ)
දෙන්	දෙන cow	දෙන්නු	දෙන්නු (පෙරරූසඳ)
හොර	හොරා thief		හොරු (පෙරසරලොප්සඳ)
වඳුරු	වැඳිරි ape (female)		වැඳිරියෝ (අගම්සඳ)
පණු	පණුවා worm		පණුවෝ (අගම්සඳ)

38. Of some masculine nouns the stem stands for the plural.

EXAMPLES. උදාහරණ.

Stem	Singular	Plural
නයි	නයා cobra	නයි
නරි	නරියා fox	නරි
හරක්	හරකා ox	හරක්
අලි	අලියා elephant	අලි

39. The plural of the following words are formed differently

Stem	Singular		Plural
ගිරා	ගිරවා	parrot	ගිරව්
රදා	රදවා	dobby	රදව්
පරා	පරවා	a fish	පරව්
ළමා	ළමයා	boy	ළමය්

40. "වර" is inserted between the stem and the case-affix, both in the Singular and the plural, to convey respect as in ගුරුවරයා teacher, ගුරුවරයෝ teachers.

EXERCISE VII. 7 අභ්‍යාස පාඩම.

(*a*) Give the plural forms of the following singular nouns :

වෙදා	medical man	සතුරා	enemy
මීයා	rat	කොල්ලා	lad
හරකා	cow	පිස්සා	mad man
ඇතා	elephant	දිවියා	leopard
අශ්වයා	horse	සිංහයා	lion
මොනරා	peacock	සහෝදරයා	brother
ඇතිනි	she elephant	ගොවියා	cultivator
කොකා	crane	වලසා	bear
මිනිසා (මිනිහා)	man	ඌරා	pig
යාළුවා	friend	දිමියා	red ant
කපුටා	crow	මැඩියා	frog

(*b*) Give the plural forms of the following noun-stems.

තෝර	යක්	මැසි
ගොන්	කපුටු	කාඩ්
දෙබර	බමුණු	හුණු
වසු	සුදු	කුමර
බලු	වඩු	මෝර
බළල්	මිතුරු	පැටි

(*c*) Write down, in Sinhalese, the meaning of the following phrases :

The boys swim. The dogs bark. The girls play. The friends come. The lads drink. The cranes fly. A bear comes. The women cry. The elephants bathe. The dogs swim. The enemies run. The monkeys descend. The boys write. The men read. The cats walk. The women sew. The medical man goes. The peacocks dance. The friends read. The leopards kill. The parrots fly.

(*d*) Write down, in English, the meanings of the following phrases :

ඌරෝ හාරනවා. ඇත්තු කනවා. මීයෝ දුවනවා. කපුටෝ පියාඹනවා. ළමයි කියවනවා. ගොවියෝ හානවා. යහළුවෝ සෝදනවා. ළමයි පෙරළෙනවා. හොරු දුවනවා. වලහා පනිනවා. සහෝදරයෝ එනවා. අශ්වයෙක් පීනනවා. ඇතින්නක් නානවා. කොකෙක් පියාඹනවා. බැළලී වැටෙනවා. මිනිස්සු හාරනවා. රිළව් වැටෙනවා.

LESSON VIII. 8 පාඩම.

FORMATION OF PLURAL. (Continued.)

Animate Nouns. ප්‍රාණවාචක ශබ්ද.

41 "වරු" is a plural termination denoting respect, and is suffixed both to masculine and feminine nouns, as in රජවරු kings, බිසෝවරු queens.

42 The plural termination ලා is generally suffixed to nouns of kindred and also to pronouns of the 2nd and 3rd persons, as in මාමලා uncles, නැන්දලා aunts, උඹලා you. තිලා you (feminine), ඌලා they (masculine), ඇලා they (feminine)

43. Words like දෙවියෝ god, රජ්ජුරුවෝ king, are honorific plurals, being plural in form but singular in signification

44. The particles ආණ, අණු, ඇණි, අණි are inserted between the stem and the case-suffix ඕ, when respect is intended to be conveyed.

ආණ and අණු are inserted in masculine nouns, and ඇණි in feminine nouns.

EXAMPLES. උදාහරණ.

පිය	+	ආණ	=	පියාණ	+	ඕ	=	පියාණෝ	father
පුත්	+	අණු	=	පුතණු	+	ඕ	=	පුතුණුවෝ	son
මා	+	ඇණි	=	මෑණි	+	ඕ	=	මෑණියෝ	mother
දූ	+	අණි	=	දුවණි	+	ඕ	=	දුවණියෝ	daughter

The Plural of the following nouns may be expressed by adding either ලා or වරු

අක්කා	elder sister	කුඩම්මා	aunt
අයියා	elder brother	බෑනා	nephew
නෑනා	sister in-law	නගා	younger sister
මස්සිනා	brother in-law	අම්මා	mother

EXERCISE VIII 8 අභ්‍යාස පාඩම.

(*a*) Give the plural forms of the nouns of which the stems are given below, inserting the honorific suffix ආණ, before the case termination ඕ.

රජ king, ගිරා parrot, මිත්‍ර friend, දරු child, වෙළෙඳ merchant, කොක් crane, මොණර peacock, උත්තම great one

(*b*) Write down, in English, the meanings of the following phrases:

අක්කාලා එනවා. ගිරාණෝ පියාඹනවා. මොණරාණෝ නටනවා. දුවණියෝ මහනවා. අම්මාලා බනිනවා. නෑනාවරු විකුණනවා. වෙළෙඳාණෝ කියවනවා. පියවරු ගහනවා. දුවණියෝ අඬනවා. මාමාලා නගිනවා. රජවරු බනිනවා. උඹලා දුවනවා. රජාණෝ නානවා. නැන්දාලා කපනවා.

LESSON IX. පාඩම.

8. FORMATION OF THE PLURAL OF INANIMATE NOUNS.

45. If the stem of an inanimate noun ends in a cerebral letter (ට, ඩ, ණ, ර, ළ,) with the inherent vowel අ the plural is generally formed by adding වල් to the stem.

In other cases the plural is the same as the stem.

EXAMPLES. උදාහරණ.

Stem.	Singular.		Plural.
කට	කට	mouth	කටවල්
බඩ	බඩ	belly	බඩවල්
පණ	පණ	life	පණවල්
ගෙදර	ගෙදර	home	ගෙදරවල්
පාර	පාර	road	පාරවල්
වළ	වළ	pit	වළවල්
රෙදි	රෙද්ද	cloth	රෙදි
කඩු	කඩුව	sword	කඩු
කන්	කන	ear	කන්
හැඳි	හැන්ද	spoon	හැඳි
කඳු	කන්ද	mountain	කඳු
ළින්	ළිඳ	well	ළින්
වළන්	වළඳ	pan	වළන්
හුළං	හුළඟ	wind	හුළං
කඹ	කඹෙ	rope	කඹ

EXCEPTIONS:—

ඇඳ	ඇඳ	bed	ඇඳන්
කඳ	කඳ	trunk	කඳන්
ගං, ගඟ	ගඟ	river	ගඟවල්

Note:—"වල්", from වන forest, has evidently been the general plural termination of inanimate nouns. In most of the nouns it has dropped from the nominative plural, but is retained in oblique cases, as in කන්වලට to the ears; වැව් වලින් from tanks; ගස්වල on the trees.

46. Names of animal, vegetable and mineral productions, such as the following, convey a plural idea.

EXAMPLES. උදාහරණ.

කිරි	milk	හාල්	unboiled rice	රන්	gold
ලේ	blood	බත්	boiled rice	රිදී	silver
මස්	flesh	තෙල්	oil	තඹ	copper
පස්	earth	වී	paddy	යකඩ	iron
පිදුරු	straw	අළු	ashes	රා	toddy
වතුර	water	වැලි	sand	මිණිරන්	plumbago
තණ	grass	පැණි	honey	අරක්කු	arraek

47. Abstract nouns expressing qualities, virtues, vices &c do not generally admit of plural, as මහත size, සීතල cold නුවණ wisdom සනීප health, ඝනකම thickness, නිදිමත sleepiness.

9. PRONOUNS. සර්වනාම.

Singular		Plural	
මම	I	අපි	we
උඹ	you	උඹලා	you
තෝ	you (disrespectful)	තොපි	you
තී	you (fem:) (do)	තොපි, තීලා	you
තමුසේ	you	තමුසේලා	you
තමුන්නාන්සේ	you (respetful)	තමුන්නාන්සේලා	you
ඔහු	he	ඔහු, ඔව්හු	they
ඌ	he (disrespectful)	ඌලා	they
උන්නැහේ	he (respectful)	උන්නැහේලා	they
උන්නාන්සේ	he (do)	උන්නාන්සේලා	they
ඈ	she	ඈලා	they
ඒකී	she (disrespectful)	ඒකීලා	they
ඒක	it	ඒවා	they

48. Many nouns signifying the doer of an action are formed by affixing කාර (කරු) to the stem of the word denoting the action, as in වැඩකාරයා, man servant.

49. Verbal nouns denoting the agent are formed by adding අන්නා to the root, as in කරන්නා, doer.

The feminine singular of the above two classes of nouns are formed by adding ඊ, as in වැඩකාරි, maid servant; කරන්නී doer.

50. Nouns signifying the mere existence of action or suffering are formed by affixing නු, ඊම, උම, ඉල්ල, or ම * to the root.

In adding these terminations the initial vowels of the root are changed in terms of rule 32. Ex: සාදනු, සෑදීම, සෑදුම, or සෑදිල්ල, the making, from සාදනවා to make; ඇදීම, ඇදුම, ඇදිල්ල, the dragging, from අදිනවා to drag; කෑම the eating or the food, from කනවා to eat

---

EXERCISE IX. 9. අගණස පාඩම.

(*a*) Write down the plural of the following singular nouns.

ඔරුව	boat	අත	hand	පිහියේ	knife
කුඩේ	umbrella	මල	flower	මැණික	gem
ඇළ	canal	දොළ	brook	පව	sin
ගහ (ගස)	tree	රළ	wave	පැදුර	mat
නැව	ship	දණ	knee	මූණ	face
වේල්ල	dam	කඩේ	boutique	යතුර	key

(*b*) Write down, in English, the meaning of the following:—

කඩකාරයා, පව්කාරයා, ඔරුකාරයා, හිරකාරයා, වතුකාරයා, බොන්නා, දුවන්නා, පනින්නා, නටන්නී, මහන්නෝ, විකිනීම, ඇඩීම, වැපිරීම, වපුරන්නෝ, මැවිල්ල, ඇල්ලීම, බැනීම, පිනීම, පිනන්නී, ගැනීම, සෙල්ලම්කරන්නෝ, බොරුකියන්නෝ, බොරුකාරයෝ.

---

* ම is added to the monosyllabic roots only.

LESSON X. 10 පාඩම.

10. Accusative Case. කම්මවිභත්තිය.

51. In animate nouns the Accusative Singular is the same as the nominative singular. but the plural generally ends in අන්, උන්, or න්, as in ගවයන්, මිනිසුන්, නයින්,

Note:—In the colloquial language the suffix ව is frequently added after the accusative termination in animate nouns, as in මිනිහාව, මිනිසුන්ව.

52. In inanimate nouns the Accusative Singular and Plural are generally the same as the nominative Singular and plural respectively, but the accusative when governed by a verb of motion towards a place, takes the termination ට.

53. The accusative comes before the verb by which it is governed.

EXERCISE X. අභ්‍යාස පාඩම·

Translate the following sentences into English :—

බල්ලෝ මීයන් මරනවා. ඇතා අත්ත කඩනවා. වඩුවෝ ගෙවල් සාදනවා. කොල්ලෝ බළලුන් මරනවා. මිනිහෙක් ගස් කපනවා කපුටෝ පණුවන් කනවා. යහළුවෝ හොරුන් අල්ලනවා. හොරා වේල්ල කඩනවා. මිනිස්සු වැව් හාරනවා. දිවියෙක් ගොනාව මරනවා. එළුවෝ කොළ කනවා. රදව් රෙදි සෝදනවා. මිනිස්සු ඔරු පදිනවා. ගොවියෝ කුඹුරු හානවා. රිළවා ගහට නගිනවා. යහළුවා ළිඳක් හාරනවා. හොරා ගසට නඟිනවා. ගැනු කඩෙට යනවා.

Translate the following sentences:—

A man ploughs the field. The old man cuts the trees. The cat catches the rat. The uncle beats the lads. The woman drags the dogs. An enemy breaks the fence. The sister-in-law weaves the mat. The dogs drink the milk.

The elder sister reads the letters. The aunt measures the thread The carpenter makes a box. She cuts the root. He digs a well. The cat rushes into the house. The uncle goes to the village.

LESSON XI. 11 පාඩම.

11. FORMATION OF THE PAST TENSE.

54. Verbs may be divided into four classes or conjugations.

55 The past tense is formed by suffixing the vowel ආ to the root. In suffixing ආ the initial vowel of the root is changed, as shewn in rule 32.

56. The roots of verbs of the 1st conjugation end in අ. In forming their past tense the vowel උ is inserted between the root and the tense-affix ආ. Thus මරනවා kill, මැරුවා killed.

The process explained:--

මර + උ + ආ.

(by changing the initial vowel අ into ඇ (rule 32) මර=මැර
(by පෙරසරලොප්සඳ) මැර + උ=මැරු
(by අගම් සඳ) මැරු + ආ=මැරුවා.

57. In trisyllables the middle vowel ආ is changed into ඇ Thus වදුරනවා say, වැදූරුවා said.

58. The past tense of some verbs of the 1st conjugation ending in ර has two forms. Ex:

Present		Past.	
කරනවා	to do	කළා	කෙරුවා
අතුරනවා	to spread	අතුළා	ඇතුරුවා
දිවරනවා	to swear	දිව්ළා,	දිවුරුවා
වගුරනවා	to shed	වගුළා,	වැගුරුවා
වදුරනවා	to say	වදුළා,	වැදූරුවා
විචාරනවා	to enquire	විචාළා,	විචැරුවා

59. The roots of verbs of the 2nd conjugation end in ආ. They do not take the vowel උ before the tense-affix ආ.

EXAMPLES උදාහරණ

Root.		Present.	Past.
හා		හානවා	හෑවා
කා	to eat	කනවා	කෑවා
දා	to burn	දනවා	දෑවා
ලා	to place	ලනවා	ලෑවා

60. The following roots of the 2nd conjugation form their past tense irregularly.

Root.		Present.	Past.
යා	to go	යනවා	ගියා
පා	to drink	බොනවා	බීවා
දා	to give	දෙනවා	දුන්නා

61. The roots of verbs of the 3rd conjugation end in ඉ. The characteristic peculiarity of this conjugation is the reduplication of the final consonant of the root before the tense-affix ආ. Thus අදිනවා drag, ඇද්දා dragged; බනිනවා abuse, බැන්නා abused.

62. If the final ඉ of the root is incorporated with a cerebral letter (ර, ළ, ට, ඩ,) the consonant is not generally reduplicated, but the letter ය is inserted between the root and the tense affix ආ. Ex.

Present.		Past.
අරිනවා	send	ඇරියා
කෙළිනවා	play	කෙළියා
සිටිනවා	stand	සිටියා
වඩිනවා	go (respectful)	වැඩියා
Exception :- කටිනවා	spin	කැට්ටා

63. If the final ඉ of the root is incorporated with the conjunct letter ඟ, ඳ, or ඹ the semi-nasal is separated and written in full. Thus නඟිනවා, ascend, නැංගා ascended. වඳිනවා worship, වැන්දා worshiped. පිඹිනවා blow, පිම්බා blew.

64. The letter ග when reduplicated assumes the form ස. Thus බඟිනවා descend, බැස්සා descended.

65. The past form of the following verbs are obsolete :— නවතිනවා stop, පවතිනවා last, වදිනවා hit against, වරදිනවා err, නිදියෙනවා sleep, වටිනවා is worth.

66. The forms නැවතුණා, පැවතුණා, වැදුණා and වැරදුණා are the past tenses of the involitive forms නැවතෙනවා, පැවතෙනවා, වැදෙනවා, and වැරදෙනවා නිදාගත්තා slept, is the past tense of නිදාගන්නවා, sleep.

The following form their past tense irregularly:—

Present.		Past.
උපදිනවා	to be born	උපන්නා
ගන්නවා	take	ගත්තා
ඉන්නවා	is	උන්නා
එනවා	come	ආවා

67. The involitive verbs are of the 4th conjugation. In this conjugation the vowel අ or ඉ of the root is changed into එ in the present tense, and the past is formed by adding උණා to the root.

EXAMPLES. උදාහරණ.

Root.		Present.	Past.
මර	to die	මැරෙනවා	මැරුණා
වා	to become	වෙනවා	වුණා, උණා

EXERCISE XI. 11 අභ්‍යාස පාඩම.

Give the past tense of the following verbs of the present tense :—

නානවා	to bathe	උදුරනවා	to snatch
උයනවා	to coock	සැනසෙනවා	to be consoled
පදිනවා	to row	ලබනවා	to receive
ගානවා	to rub	පිහිනවා	to sweep
කියනවා	to say	අඹරනවා	to twist
ලියනවා	to write	පාගනවා	to trample upon
පිපිරෙනවා	to burst	කොටනවා	to cut, to dig
ලැබෙනවා	to obtain	කියවනවා	to read
කහිනවා	to cough	පුළුස්සනවා	to burn
හාරනවා	to dig	සනසනවා	to console
බබලනවා	to shine	කොඳුරනවා	to whisper
වැවෙනවා	to grow	ඉදිමෙනවා	to swell
ඉපදෙනවා	to be born	වහිනවා	to rain
බදිනවා	to fry	වියනවා	to weave
දිවුරනවා	to swear	සොරකම් කරනවා	to steal

Translate the following sentences :—

අපි ලිඳක් හෑරුවා. කොල්ලෝ වලන් බින්දා. මස්සිනා කඹ අඹරනවා. අයියා ගහ කැපුවා. බල්ලා ඌරුව මරුවා. ඇතින්න අතු කඩනවා. යහළුවෝ වැට බැන්දා. සතුරෝ නියර කැඩුවා. ඌ රෙදි සොරකම්කළා. පිඟියේ කැඩුණා. මූ රා බීවා. ගල පිපිරෙනවා. ළමයෙක් උපන්නා. ගොන්නු පිදුරු කෑවා. මිනිස්සු බත් කෑවා. අපි මිණිරන් හාරනවා. අයියා වී වැපුරුවා. හොරු ගේ පිලිස්සුවා. ඈ දිවුරුවා. අශ්වයෝ තණ කෑවා.

LESSON XII. 12 පාඩම.

12. PARTICIPLES.

68. The present participle ends in මින් or මින, as in කරමින් doing.

· The continuation of an action is also expressed by repeating the verb, as in කරකර doing; ගහගහ beating.

69. The past participle is formed by changing the final අ of the root of the 1st conjugation into ආ, as in කපනවා cut, කපා having cut.

70. In the 2nd conjugation the past participle is the same as the root, as in කනවා eat, කා having eaten.

71 In the 3rd conjugation the final ඉ of the root is changed into අ and the initial vowel අ into ඇ; the initial ඉ remains unchanged as in බනිනවා abuse, බැන having abused; සිටිනවා stand, සිට having stood.

72. In the 4th conjugation the final එ is changed into ඊ, as in වැටෙනවා fall, වැටී having fallen.

To these past participle forms ලා is often affixed, as in කපාලා, කාලා, බැනලා, වැටීලා.

73. The following verbs form their past participle irregularly.

Present.		Past participle.
කරනවා	do	කර, කරලා, කොට
බොනවා	drink	බී, බීලා
යනවා	go	ගොස්, ගොහින්
දෙනවා	give	දී, දීලා
එනවා	come	ඇවිත්, අවුත්, ඇවිදින්
වෙනවා	become	වී, වෙලා
ගන්නවා	take	ගෙන

EXERCISE XII. 12 අභ්‍යාස පාඩම.

Give the present and past participle of the following verbs.

කථාකරනවා	speak	ලැබෙනවා	receive
උණුකරනවා	boil	වක්කරනවා	pour
මත්වෙනවා	become intoxicated	ගලනවා	flow
බනිනවා	abuse	වළලනවා	bury
සොරකම්කරනවා	steal	බඳිනවා	bind

වැඩකරනවා	work	කසාදබඳිනවා	marry
වෙඩිතිබනවා	fire at	කොල්ලකනවා	rob
සූදුකෙළිනවා	gamble	කිමිදිනවා	dive
සැඟවෙනවා	conceal	පැරදෙනවා	lose, be [defeated

Translate the following :

ඇතා නාලා කැලෙට ගියා. හොරු ගොනාව මරාලා සැඟවී ගියා. මස්සිනා ගමට ගොස් ආවා. වැඩකාරයා තැබෑරුමට ගොස් අරක්කු බීවා කොල්ලා සූදුකෙළලා පැරදුණා. ගොත්තු තණ කාලා නිදියෙනවා. මූ රා බීලා මත් වුණා. ඔව්හු කසාදබැඳලා ගමට ගියා. වැඩකාරයා බඩු සොරකම්කරගෙන සැඟවිලා ඉන්නවා. මාමා වෙඩිතිබාලා අශ්වයා මැරුවා. ඌ රා බීලා වැටි වැටී ගියා. මිනිස්සු කථා කර කර ඇවිදිනවා. බල්ලෝ දුවමින් බුරනවා. වැඩකාරී බැන බැන යනවා.

LESSON XIII. 13 පාඩම.

13. Instrumental Case. කතෘවිභක්ති.

74. The termination of the instrumental case are the same as those of the accusative, with the exception of ට.

75. The particle විසින්, by, is often used after the instrumental case, as in මා විසින් දුන් කාසි, the money given by me.

76. The Particles සහ, හා, සමග, කැටුව, signifying with, govern a noun in the instrumental case, as in මා සමග, with me ; ඒ මිනිහා සහ මම, I with that man ; උඹ කැටුව with you.

14. Verbal Adjective. ගුණවාචක ක්‍රියා.

77. There are no relative pronouns in Sinhalese. They are conveyed by verbal adjectives.

78. The verbal adjectives present of volitive verbs generally end in අන, අන්නාවූ or න and the past in උ, ඌ, ආවූ, අපු or ආපු.

Note:—අපු and ආපු are affixed to the root only.

79. The crude form of the past tense is also used as past verbal adjective, as, ගත් taken, කළ done, ගිය gone.

EXAMPLES. උදාහරණ.

ගොනා කන තණකොළ the grass which the bull eats.
ගමට යන්නාවූ මිනිහා, the man who goes to the village.
ගොනා අදින කරත්තේ, the cart which the bull draws.
ගමට ගිය මිනිහා, the man who went to the village.
උඹ මැරූ බල්ලා, the dog which you killed.
උඹ කළාවූ වැඩේ, the work which you did.
අශ්වයා කාපු වී, the paddy which the horse ate.
පියා විසින් දුන් අවවාද, the advice given by the father.

80. In involitive verbs the present verbal adjective ends in එන and the past in උණ or උණු, as in වැවෙන ගහ, the tree which grows; වැවුණු ගහ, the tree which grew.

EXERCISE XIII. 13. අභ්‍යාස පාඩම.

Translate the following:—

(*a*) සොරු ගත් බඩු. වඩුවා සෑදූ පුටුව. මාමා කපන ගහ. ළමයා විසින් මැරූ බළලා රෑ බොන කොල්ලා. මාමා බැඳපු පොත්. වැඩකාරයා ගෙනෙන වතුර. අරක්කු බොන මිනිස්සු මේ මිනිහා කළ කතාව. පියා දීලා ගිය කාසි ළමයින් කියවන පොත්. ගොන් අදින්නාවූ කරත්තේ. දුවන අශ්වයා. අප සමග ආ ළමයි.

(*b*) The dog which barks. The letter written by the girl. The table made by the carpenter. The fruit brought by the sister. The paddy sown by us. The milk sold by the servant. The rice sold by the boutique keeper. The man who died. The field ploughed by you. The friend who gave the money.

5

LESSON XIV. 14 පාඩම.

15. Interrogative Pronouns.

කව්ද	who	කොයිබද	where
කාගේද	whose	මන්ද	why
කාටද	to whom	ඇයි	why
කාගෙන්ද	from whom	කොයි	which
කොහේද	where	කවදද	when
කෝකද	which	මොකද	what

81. ද is an interrogative particle used after finite verbs, nouns, pronouns, adverbs &c.. as in උඹ යනවාද, do you go? ළමයාද, is it the boy? මමද, is it I? අදද, is it to-day?

82. There is a participial form, which includes the verb, the relative and the noun, and is used with interrogative pronouns and the negative particle "නෑ," no, with the ellipsis of the predicate verb. This we call Relative Participle because it refers to a noun which is understood.

16. Relative Participles.

83. Relative Participles, present singular, are formed by suffixing අන්නේ, or ඉන්නේ to the roots of volitive verbs and එන්නේ to those of involitive verbs, as in කරන්නේ one who does; සිටින්නේ one who stands; වැටෙන්නේ one who falls.

84. Relative Participles, past singular, are formed by suffixing ඒ to the root of the past tense in volitive verbs and උණේ in involitive verbs, as in සිටියේ he who stood; වැටුණේ he who fell.

85. The plural of relative participles is formed by suffixing ඕ to the singular, as in සිටින්නෝ, සිටියෝ &c.

EXAMPLES. උදාහරණ.

වැඩේ කරන්නේ කව්ද, who is doing the work.
(lit. who is the work doing one)

බල්ලා කෑවේ මොනවාද, what did the dog eat.
(lit what was the thing of which the dog was an eater)

අශ්වයා දුවන්නේ නෑ, the horse does not run
(lit. the horse is not a running one)

EXERCISE XIV. 14 අභ්‍යස පාඩම.

Translate the foolowing:—

වැඩකාරයා ගියේ කොහේද? රදවා මැරුණේ කවදාද? කිරි ගෙනාවේ කව්ද? බල්ලෝ බුරන්නේ කාටද? ළමයා කියන්නේ මොකද? වැට කැඩුවේ කව්ද? හොරු දිව්වේ කොහේද? අයියා බත් කෑවේ නෑ. නංගි බැන්නේ කාටද? එළුවා වතුර බොන්නේ නෑ. උඹ ගහ කැපුවේ මන්ද? උඹ ආවේ ඇයි?

What does the man say? Where did you go? Who killed the bear? Did the dhoby come? The carpenter does not make the chair. Did the man bring the box? Why does not the boy write the letter? Who is beating the blind man? Why did you kill the cat. I did not take the money.

LESSON XV. 15 පාඩම.

17. AUXILIARY CASE. කරණ විභක්ති.

86. The auxilary case generally ends in ඉන් or එන්.

EXAMPLES. උදාහරණ.

Singular		Plural	
අතින්	with the hand	අත්වලින්	with hands
ගලකින්	with a stone	ගල්වලින්	with stones
පොල්ලෙන්	with the club	පොලුවලින්	with clubs

18. DATIVE CASE. සම්ප්‍රදාන විභක්ති.

අට, ලොවට	to the world	අන්ට, දරුවන්ට	to the children
ආට, හොරාට	to the thief	උන්ට, සොරුන්ට	to the thieves
උට, රජුට	to the king	න්ට, අලින්ට	to the elephants
හට, රජහට	to the king		
ට, මට	to me		

EXERCISE XV. 15 අභ්‍යාස පාඩම.

Translate the following :—

හොරා මටපොල්ලෙන් ගැහුවා. වැඩකාරි ළමයින්ට කෑම දුන්නා. මස්සිනා හොරාට පිහියෙන් ඇන්නා. උඹ පිහියෙන් ගහ කැපුවා. අයියා ගොනාට පයින් ගැහුවා. මාමා සොරුන්ට බැන්නා. නංගි පෑනෙන් ලියුවා. අම්මා වැඩකාරයින්ට බත් දුන්නා. කොල්ලෝ කඹෙන් ගොනාව බැන්දා. මම පයින් ගියා. අයියා මට පොතක් දුන්නා.

The son with his hand took the flowers. The thief burnt the house with fire. The woman gave me water. The father beat the servant with a stick. The thief stabbed the woman with the knife. I gave a cloth to the blindman The boy gave me toddy

LESSON XVI. 16 පාඩම.

19. ABLATIVE CASE. අවධි විභක්ති.

Singular.

අගෙන්, මවගෙන්	from the mother
ආගෙන්, සොරාගෙන්	from the thief
උගෙන්, සොරුගෙන්	from the thief
ඉන්, ගසින්	from the tree
එන්, පොළොවෙන්	from the earth

Plural.

අන්ගෙන්, සතුරන්ගෙන්	from the enemies
ඉන්ගෙන්, ගොවින්ගෙන්	from the cultivators
උන්ගෙන්, මහතුන්ගෙන්	from the gentlemen
න්ගෙන්, ස්ත්‍රීන්ගෙන්	from the women.

20. GENITIVE CASE. සම්බන්ධ විභක්ති.

Singular.

අගේ,	බිසවගේ	of the queen
ආගේ,	සර්පයාගේ	of the serpent
උගේ,	රජුගේ	of the king
හුගේ,	වෙළඳහුගේ	of the merchant.

Plural.

අන්ගේ,	මනුෂ්‍යයන්ගේ	of the men
උන්ගේ,	සොරුන්ගේ	of the thieves

Note:—These genitive terminations are affixed only to animate nouns. In inanimate nouns the genitive terminations are the same as the locative.

21. LOCATIVE CASE. ආධාර විභක්ති.

Singular.			Plural.		
එහි,	අහසෙහි	in the sky	අන්හි,	වෘක්ෂයන්හි	in the trees
ඒ,	ගහේ	in the tree	වලැ,	ගස්වලැ	in the trees
ති,	සිත්හි	in the mind			
ඇ,	නුවරැ	in the city			

Note:—These locative terminations are used only after inanimate nouns. In animate nouns the termination කෙරෙහි is affixed, as in මිනිහා කෙරෙහි in the man.

22. VOCATIVE CASE. ආලපන විභක්ති.

Singular			Plural.		
අ,	එළුවා	O goat	ඉනි,	කිවිනි	O poets
ආ,	ගිරවා	O parrot	එනි,	දරුවෙනි	O children
ඒ,	නැන්දේ	O aunt	උනි,	ගිරවුනි	O parrots
ඕ,	වඩුවෝ	O carpenter	අනෙ,	දරුවනෙ	O children

EXERCISE XVI. 16 අභ්‍යාස පාඩම.

Translate the following:—

වැඩකාරයා මහත්මයාගේ පෙට්ටියෙන් කාසි ගත්තා. මිනිහෙක් කඩෙන් බඩු ගත්තා. හොරා ගහෙන් බැසලා කැලේට

දිව්වා. කොල්ලෙක් පාරේ සිටිනවා. ගොවියා කුඹුරේ වි වපුරනවා. බබද්දො තැබැරුමෙන් අරක්කු බොනවා මම සොරුන්ට වෙඩි තිබ්බා. කඩකාරයන්ගේ ගෙවල් සොරු ගිනි තිබ්බා. වඩුවෝ වත්තේ කතාකරකර සිටිනවා. ඌව ගමින් ගෙනා රා කොල්ලා බීවා.

The woman, having taken rice from the boutique, went to the village. The monkey fell from the tree The men are working in the tank. The boy stole the carpenter's goods. The cat drank the children's milk. I borrowed money from the woman. The bird which was brought by the maidservant died. I drank the water of the tank. I gave food to the dogs. The thief, whom I caught, jumped into the well.

LESSON XVII. 17 පාඩම.

23. Imperatine Mood. විධික්‍රියා.

Terminations.

බලනවා to look; සිටිනවා to stand.

Singular.		Plural.	
අ,	බල	අව්,	බලව්
අව,	බලව		
උ,	සිටු	ඉව්,	සිටිව්
අන්	බලන්		
ඉන්,	සිටින්		
පන්,	බලාපන්, සිටපන්	පල්ලා,	බලාපල්ලා, සිටපල්ලා
පිය,	බලාපිය, සිටපිය	පියව්,	බලාපියව්, සිටපියව්
අන්න,	බලන්න		
ඉන්න,	සිටින්න		

Note:—In affixing පිය, පන් පියව් and පල්ලා the final අ of the root is often changed into ආ, but there are many words which retain the short vowel, අ, as in කරපිය do, ගහපිය beat, පැනපිය jump &c.

87. The imperative with the terminations පිය or පියව් is disrespectful, and is used with the pronouns තෝ and තොපි, as in තෝ කරපිය, තොපි කරපියව්.

88. Terminations පන් and පල්ලා express familiarity and are used with the pronouns උඹ and උඹලා, as in උඹකරපන්, උඹලා කරපල්ලා.

89. The termination අන්න is honorific and is generally used with the pronoun තමුසේ or තමුන්නාන්සේ, as in තමුසේ යන්න, තමුන්නාන්සේ යන්න, you go.

90. The particle මැනවි with a gerundival or conditional particle is also used as an imperative denoting respect, as in ලියනු මැනවි please write, වඩිනා මැනවි please go or come

91. The imperative forms of some verbs are irregular.

EXAMPLES. උදාහරණ.

Verb.		Imperative Singular.	Imperative Plural.
යනවා	to go	පල, පලයන්	පලයව්, පලයල්ලා
එනවා	to come	වර, වරෙන්	වරෙව්, වරෙල්ලා
දෙනවා	to give	දිය, දියන්, දීපිය, දීපන්.	දියව්, දියල්ලා, දීපියව්, දීපල්ලා

Note:—දිය and දියන් and their plural දියව් and දියල්ලා mean "give me" or "give us." දීපන් and දීපිය and their plural දීපල්ලා and දීපියව් mean "give to others."

EXERCISE XVII. 17 අභ්‍යාස පාඩම.

Translate the following:—

ළමයිනි ගෙදර පලයල්ලා. මාමේ මට පොතක් දියන්. තමුසේ පුටුවෙහිවාඩි වෙන්න. තෝ වැඩකාරයාගේ පිහි යේ දීපිය. උඹ ස්කෝලයට පලයන්. තෝ ස්කෝලයට පල. තමුන්නාන්සේ ලියමන ලියන්න. තොපි ගගේ අතු කපව. තෝ වතුර බොපිය. අක්කේ උඹ රෙද්ද මහපන්. කොල්ලෝ

තෝ බත් කාපිය. මහත්මයා වැඩකාරයින්ට කෑම දෙන්න: තෝ කරත්තේ සෝදාපිය. අඩියේ උඹ ගෙදර වරෙන්. බල්ලාට කෑම දීපිය.

Boy, take this letter to the Post Office. Open this box. Sir, give me a rupee. Give this money to the dhoby. Carpenter, make me a chair. Dig a pit in the garden. Friend, give me the book which you took from the uncle. Children, you go to the garden. Boys, run home.

24. Declension.

Animate Nouns.

Stem ending in Vowels.

වැදි, hunter.

	Singular.	Plural.
Nom.	වැද්දා	වැද්දෝ
Acc.	වැද්දා	වැද්දන්
Instr.	වැද්දා	වැද්දන්
Dat.	වැද්දාට	වැද්දන්ට
Abl.	වැද්දාගෙන්	වැද්දන්ගෙන්
Gen.	වැද්දාගේ	වැද්දන්ගේ
Loc.	වැද්දා කෙරෙහි	වැද්දන් කෙරෙහි
Voc.	වැද්දා, වැද්දෝ	වැද්දුනි

දිමි, red ant.

	Singular.	Plural.
Nom.	දිමියා	දිමියෝ
Acc.	දිමියා	දිමියන්
Instr.	දිමියා	දිමියන්
Dat.	දිමියාට	දිමියන්ට
Abl.	දිමියාගෙන්	දිමියන්ගෙන්
Gen.	දිමියාගේ	දිමියන්ගේ
Loc.	දිමියා කෙරෙහි	දිමියන් කෙරෙහි
Voc.	දිමියා, දිමියෝ	දිමියනි

කොලු. lad.

	Singular.	Plural.
Nom.	කොල්ලා	කොල්ලෝ
Acc.	කොල්ලා	කොල්ලන්
Instr.	කොල්ලා	කොල්ලන්
Dat.	කොල්ලාට	කොල්ලන්ට
Abl.	කොල්ලාගෙන්	කොල්ලන්ගෙන්
Gen.	කොල්ලාගේ	කොල්ලන්ගේ
Loc.	කොල්ලා කෙරෙහි	කොල්ලන් කෙරෙහි
Voc.	කොල්ලා, කොල්ලෝ	කොල්ලනි

වඩු. carpenter.

	Singular.	Plural.
Nom.	වඩුවා	වඩුවෝ
Acc.	වඩුවා	වඩුවන්
Instr.	වඩුවා	වඩුවන්
Dat.	වඩුවාට	වඩුවන්ට
Abl.	වඩුවාගෙන්	වඩුවන්ගෙන්
Gen.	වඩුවාගේ	වඩුවන්ගේ.
Loc.	වඩුවා කෙරෙහි	වඩුවන් කෙරෙහි
Voc.	වඩුවා, වඩුවෝ	වඩුවනි

ලිය. woman.

	Singular.	Plural.
Nom.	ලිය	ලියෝ
Acc.	ලිය	ලියන්
Instr.	ලිය	ලියන්
Dat.	ලියට	ලියන්ට
Abl.	ලියගෙන්	ලියන්ගෙන්
Gen.	ලියගේ	ලියන්ගේ
Loc.	ලියකෙරෙහි	ලියන්කෙරෙහි
Voc.	ලිය, ලියේ	ලියනි

හොර. thief.

	Singular.	Plural.
Nom.	හොරා	හොරු
Acc.	හොරා	හොරුන්
Instr.	හොරා	හොරුන්
Dat.	හොරාට	හොරුන්ට
Abl.	හොරාගෙන්	හොරුන්ගෙන්
Gen.	හොරාගේ	හොරුන්ගේ
Loc.	හොරා කෙරෙහි	හොරුන් කෙරෙහි
Voc.	හොරා	හොරුනි

ළමා. boy.

	Singular.	Plural.
Nom.	ළමයා	ළමය්
Acc.	ළමයා	ළමයින්
Instr	ළමයා	ළමයින්
Dative.	ළමයාට	ළමයින්ට
Abl.	ළමයාගෙන්	ළමයින්ගෙන්
Gen.	ළමයාගේ	ළමයින්ගේ
Loc.	ළමයා කෙරෙහි	ළමයින් කෙරෙහි
Voc.	ළමයා, ළමයෝ	ළමයිනි

නැඳෑ. aunt.

	Singular.	Plural.
Nom.	නැන්දෑ	නැන්දෑලා
Acc.	නැන්දෑ	නැන්දෑලා
Instr.	නැන්දෑ	නැන්දෑලා
Dat.	නැන්දෑට	නැන්දෑලාට
Abl.	නැන්දෑගෙන්	නැන්දෑලාගෙන්
Gen.	නැන්දෑගේ	නැන්දෑලාගේ
Loc.	නැන්දෑ කෙරෙහි	නැන්දෑලා කෙරෙහි
Voc.	නැන්දෑ, නැන්දේ	නැන්දෑලා

Stem ending in a mute consonant.

පුත්. son.

	Singular.	Plural.
Nom.	පුතා	පුත්හු, පුත්තු
Acc.	පුතා	පුතුන්
Instr.	පුතා	පුතුන්
Dat.	පුතාට	පුතුන්ට
Abl.	පුතාගෙන්	පුතුන්ගෙන්
Gen.	පුතාගේ	පුතුන්ගේ
Loc.	පුතාකෙරෙහි	පුතුන් කෙරෙහි
Voc.	පුතා, පුතේ	පුතුනි

Inanimate Nouns.

Stem ending in a vowel,

පාර. road.

	Singular.	Plural.
Nom.	පාර	පාරවල්
Acc.	පාර	පාරවල්
Aux.	පාරෙන්	පාරවලින්
Dat.	පාරට	පාරවලට
Abl.	පාරෙන්	පාරවලින්
Gen.	පාරේ	පාරවල
Loc.	පාරෙහි, පාරේ	පාරවල

Stem ending in a mute consonant.

ගස්. trees.

	Singnlar.	Plural.
Nom.	ගස	ගස්
Acc.	ගස	ගස්
Aux.	ගසින්	ගස්වලින්
Dat.	ගසට	ගස්වලට
Abl.	ගසින්	ගස්වලින්
Gen.	ගසේ	ගස්වල
Loc.	ගසෙහි, ගසේ	ගස්වල

25 PRONOUNS.

First Person. Common Gender.

මා, I.

	Singular.	Plural.
Nom.	මම	අපි
Acc.	මා	අප
Instr.	මා	අප
Dat.	මට	අපට
Abl.	මගෙන්	අපෙන්, අපගෙන්
Gen.	මගේ, මාගේ	අපේ, අපගේ
Loc.	මා කෙරෙහි	අප කෙරෙහි

Second Person. Masculine Gender.

තා, thou, you.

	Singular.	Plural.
Nom.	තෝ	තොපි
Acc.	තා	තොප
Instr.	තා	තොප
Dat.	තට	තොපට
Abl.	තගෙන්, තාගෙන්	තොපෙන්, තොපගෙන්
Gen.	තගේ, තාගේ	තොපේ, තොපගේ
Loc.	තා කෙරෙහි	තොප කෙරෙහි

Second Person. Feminine Gender.

තී, thou, you.

	Singular.	Plural.
Nom.	තී	තොපි, තීලා
Acc.	තී	තොප, තීලා
Instr.	තී	තොප, තීලා
Dat.	තිට	තොපට, තීලාට
Abl.	තිගෙන්, තීගෙන්	තොපගෙන්, තීලාගෙන්
Gen.	තීගේ, තිගේ	තොපගේ, තීලාගේ
Loc.	තී කෙරෙහි	තොප තීලා } කෙරෙහි

Second Persod. Common Gender.

උඹ. You.

	Singular.	Plural.
Nom.	උඹ	උඹලා
Acc.	උඹ	උඹලා
Instr.	උඹ	උඹලා
Dat.	උඹට	උඹලාට
Abl.	උඹෙන්, උඹගෙන්	උඹලාගෙන්
Gen.	උඹේ, උඹගේ	උඹලාගේ
Loc.	උඹ කෙරෙහි	උඹලා කෙරෙහි

Third Person. Masculine Gender.

ඒ, උ. He.

	Singular.	Plural.
Nom.	ඒ, ඔහු	ඔව්හු, ඔහු
Acc.	ඔහු, ඌ	ඔවුන්, උන්
Instr	ඔහු, ඌ	ඔවුන්, උන්
Dat.	ඔහුට, ඌට	ඔවුන්ට, උන්ට
Abl.	ඔහුගෙන්, ඌගෙන්	ඔවුන්ගෙන්, උන්ගෙන්
Gen.	ඔහුගේ, ඌගේ	ඔවුන්ගේ, උන්ගේ
Loc.	ඔහු කෙරෙහි, ඌ කෙරෙහි	ඔවුන් කෙරෙහි, උන් කෙරෙහි

Third Person. Feminine Gender

ඈ, ඕ. She.

	Singular.	Plurrl.
Nom.	ඈ, ඕ	ඔහු, ඔව්හු
Acc.	ඈ, ඇය	ඔවුන්
Instr.	ඈ, ඇය	ඔවුන්
Dat.	ඈට, ඇයට	ඔවුන්ට
Abl.	ඈගෙන්, ඇයගෙන්	ඔවුන්ගෙන්
Gen.	ඈගේ, ඇගේ, ඇයගේ	ඔවුන්ගේ
Loc.	ඈ කෙරෙහි	ඔවුන් කෙරෙහි

Third Person. Neuter Gender.

එ. it.

	Singular.	Plural
Nom.	එය, ඒක	ඒවා .
Acc.	එය, ඒක	ඒවා
Aux.	එයින්, ඒකෙන්	ඒවායින්
Dat.	එයට, ඒකට	ඒවාට
Abl.	එයින්, ඒකෙන්	ඒවායින්
Gen.	ඒකේ	ඒවායේ
Loc.	එහි	ඒවායේ

EXERCIE XVIII. අටළොස පාඩම.

Translate the following:—

අශ්වයා මගේ කරත්තේ කැඩුවා. කොල්ලෝ උන්ට උඹ දීපු කාසි නැතිකළා. හරක් වැට බිඳලා ඇවිත් වත්තේ තණකොළ කෑවා. මගේ යාළුවා උඹලාගේ ගෙදර සිටි එළුවා මැරුවා. ඒක උඹට දුන්නේ කව්ද? ඈ මට බත් උයලා දුන්නා. ඔහුට සීනි දුන්නේ කව්ද? මගේ වැඩකාරයාගේ පැදුර පිලිස්සුවේ කව්ද? කුරුල්ලෝ කුඹුරේ වී කාලා පියාඹනවා. උඹ ලමයාගේ මුහුණට ගැහුවේ මන්ද? තොපි පාරේ තැබෑරුමට ගොස් අරක්කු බීවාද? ඒවායේ මම ඉනි කැපුවා. වැඩකාරයෝ උන්ගේ කඩේ හාල් සොරකම්කළා. මහත්මයාගේ වත්තේ මම ලිඳක් හෑරුවා.

Your brother cut the fence stick with my knife. I bought rice from your uncle's boutique. We construct the dam. I went to my village in a boat. My nephew stabbed the thief with his knife. Your mother gave me an umbrella. My brother-in-law took the cloth from your niece. Our dogs ate the flesh which you gave them. My friends bathe in the sea. Your grand father abused my younger brother. She came to the school. I took it from my uncle. We plough our fields. You sow paddy in your field.

LESSON XIX. 19 පාඩම.

26. ADJECTIVES.

93. Adjectives are not declined like nouns. They are prefixed, in their unaltered forms, to the nouns which they qualify.

The following list of adjectives may be committed to memory.

Vocabulary 4.

කළු,	black	දික්,	long
සුදු,	white	කොට,	short
නිල්,	blue	පටු,	narrow
රතු,	red	මිටි,	short
දුඹුරු,	brown	පහත්,	low
ලොකු,	big	උස්,	high, tall
කුඩා,	small	මහා	great
පුංචි,	small	නාකි, old	applied to animates
හොඳ,	good	මහළු, old	applied to animates
නරක,	bad	පරණ,	old, applied to things
නපුරු,	wicked	අලුත්,	new
මේ,	this	දුප්පත්,	poor
අර,	that	පොහොසත්,	rich
නීච,	mean	කීකරු,	obedient
කිලුටු,	dirty	තරුණ,	young
කොර,	lame	බාල,	young

27. THE INFINITIVE MOOD.

94. The infinative is formed by adding න්ට or න්නට to the root, as in කරන්ට or කරන්නට, to do.

28. INDECLINABLE WORDS. නිපාත.

95. Adverbs, prepositions and conjunctions come under the class නිපාත. The following is a list of indeclinable words which are most commonly used.

Vocabulary 5.

දැන්,	now	දී,	at
අද,	today	නුමුත්,	but
ඊයේ,	yesterday	සමග,	with
හෙට,	to-morrow	නිතර,	always
එවිට,	then	විසින්,	by
තවම,	yet, still	අහක,	away
එහි,	there	මෙසේ,	thus
මෙහි,	here	එසේ,	so
කොහේ,	where	නොහොත්,	or
වාගේ,	like	ඕනෑ,	must
ඔව්	yes	කොහොම,	how
නෑ,	no	එක්ක,	with
එපා,	do not, do not want	බෑ,	cannot
බොහොම,	much	ටිකක්	a little, a few
තුරු,	until	නම්,	if

Note:—බෑ follows a dative, as in මට බෑ, I cannot.

තුරු is affixed to verbal adjectives, as in උඹ එනතුරු until you come.

නම් is affixed to finite verbs, as in ඔහු එනවානම්, if he comes, ඔහු ගියානම්, if he went.

EXERCISE XIX.

Translate the following:—

මේ ගමේ දුප්පත් මිනිස්සු ගගේ මාලු අල්ලනවා. මගේ සුදු රෙද්ද බල්ලා ඉරුවා. පුංචි ළමයි වෙලේ දුවනවා. මේ නාකි මිනිහා නිතරම පාරේ ඇවිදිනවා. අද මම මගේ පරණ කරත්තේ වික්කා. උඹලා මගේ ලොකු කුඹුර හෙට හාන්ට ඕනෑ. මගේ අලුත් තොප්පිය සොරකම් කලේ කවුද? උඹේ මස්සිනා තවම ගමට ආවේ නැද්ද? උඹේ ගොනා වාගේ කළු ගොනෙක් වත්තක ඉන්නවා මම ඊයේ දැක්කා. මගේ කිලුටු රෙදි රදවාට දීපන්. මේ මිනිහාට අහක යන්ට

කියාපන්. මම මගේ මලයා සමග කුඹුරට ගියා නුමුත් ගොයම කැපුවේ නෑ. මට නාන්ට බෑ. මම ඒ වැඩේ කළා නුමුත් උඹ මට කාසි දුන්නේ නෑ.

I saw your black cow in the field. She did not come home to-day. Tell the man to bring a few fence sticks from the jungle. My grandson cut this tree with his knife. Give the dirty clothes to the dhoby. That wicked man beat this poor boy with his stick. We met your friends there. He abused the lame man. I cannot go with this little boy. This man or this woman must do the work. Tell him so. Come here, man.

LESSON XX. 20 පාඩම.

27. THE VERB TO BE, ඉන්නවා, සිටිනවා, තිබෙන්වා.

96. The verbs ඉන්නවා and සිටිනවා, to be, are used only for animates, and තිබෙනවා for inanimates.

Ex: මිනිහෙක් ඉන්නවා, there is a man
ළමයා සිටිනවා. there is the boy
පාරක් තිබෙනවා. there is a road.

97. The verb ඉන්නවා සිටිනවා or තිබෙනවා is generally omitted after an adjective, a noun, or an adverb, ending a sentence, and is then expressed by the particle යි.

Ex; මේ ළමයා නරකයි, this boy is bad [eats
ගොනා කන්නේ තණකොළයි, it is grass that the bull
ළමයා ආවේ අදයි, it is to-day that the boy came.

98. The particle ඉ is affixed to an indefinite noun ending a sentence, in order to express the verb to be Ex: මේ මිනිහා හොරෙකි, this man is a thief.

99. The verb තිබෙනවා takes the dative of a noun or pronoun signifying possessor, Ex: මට පොතක් තිබෙනවා. I have a book, lit. There is a book to me.

28. Numerals.

103. Ordinal numerals precede the nouns which they affect, as in **පළමුවෙනි මිනිහා,** the first man. When a cardinal number refers to animates that number is followed by **එක්** for the singular and **දෙනෙක්** or **දෙන** for the plural, as in **මිනිහෙක්** a man, **මිනිස්සු තුන්දෙනෙක්** three men, **මිනිස්සු තුන්දෙන,** the three men. When a cardinal number refers to inanimates **අක්** is suffixed, as in **පොත් තුනක්** three books. **පොත් තුන** means the three books.

Vocabulary 6.

Cardinal.				Ordinal.	
එක	1	හතළිස්එක	41	පළමුවෙනි	1st
දෙක	2	පනහ	50	දෙවෙනි	2nd
තුන	3	පනස්එක	51	තුන්වෙනි	3rd
හතර	4	හැට	60	හතරවෙනි	4th
පහ	5	හැටඑක	61	පස්වෙනි	5th
හය	6	හැත්තෑව	70	හයවෙනි	6th
හත	7	හත්තෑඑක	71	හත්වෙනි	7th
අට	8	අසූව	80	අටවෙනි	8th
නවය	9	අසූඑක	81	නවවෙනි	9th
දහය	10	අනූව	90	දහවෙනි	10th
එකොළහ	11	අනූඑක	91	එකොළොස්වෙනි	11th
දොළහ	12	සියය	100	දොළොස්වෙනි	12th
දහතුන	13	එකසියඑක	01	දහතුන්වෙනි	13th
දහහතර	14	දෙසිය	200	දහහතරවෙනි	14th
පහළොව	15	තුන්සිය	300	පහළොස්වෙනි	15th
දහසය	16	හාරසිය	400	දහසයවෙනි	16th
දහහත	17	පන්සිය	500	දහහත්වෙනි	17th
දහඅට	18	හයසිය	600	දහඅටවෙනි	18th
දහනවය	19	හත්සිය	700	දහනවවෙනි	19th
විස්ස	20	අටසිය	800	විසිවෙනි	20th
විසිඑක	21	නවසිය	900	තිස්වෙනි	30th
තිහ	30	දාහ	1000	හතළිස්වෙනි	40th
තිස්එක	31	එක්දාස්එක	1001	පනස්වෙනි	50th
හතළිහ	40	දෙදාහ	2000	හැටවෙනි	60th

EXERCISE XX. 20 අභ්‍යාස පාඩම.

Translate the following:—

කොල්ලා පාරේ ඉන්නවා. ගලක් මේසේ උඩ තිබෙනවා. හොරු පොල්ගෙඩි හතරක් ගෙනගියා. මම බෙල්ලන් සියයක් මිලට ගත්තා. මේසේ උඩ තිබෙන්නේ මොනවාද? අලියා සිටියේ කොහේද? ළමයි පස්දෙනෙක් වත්තේ සෙල්ලම් කරනවා. අර වෙලේ සිටින්නේ කව්ද? මේ මිනිහා මගේ සතුරෙකි. මේ සොරකම කළේ උඹයි. මේ ළමයා මගේ වලන් දෙකක් බින්දෑ. මට ළමයි දෙදෙනෙක් සිටිනවා. එන මාසේ පහළොස්වෙනි දින මම ගමට යනවා. කුඹුරේ හරක් උන්නාද? හරක් හදෙනෙක් (හය දෙනෙක්) වැට බිඳගෙන කුඹුරට ආවා. ඌ ගමට යන්නේ හෙටයි. මේ ඌරා මහළුයි.

I sold the two goats for fifty rupees. There is a bird on a branch of that tree. This table is very long There are cocoanut trees on my land. I bought three hundred arecanuts from this old man. This man is a fool. Give twentyfive cents to the dhoby. The servant went to his village on the 4th (day) of last month. I have three parrots, which I brought from the village. My dog is black.

LESSON XXI. 21 පාඩම.

29. THE CAUSAL VERB, ප්‍රයෝජ්‍ය ක්‍රියා (පියදුකිරිය).

101 The causal verb is formed by inserting ව between the root of the verb and the inflectional ending. ලවා is used after the agent. Ex. මම වැඩේ කරවනවා, I get the work done; මම වඩුවා ලවා වැඩේ කරවනවා, I get the work done by the carpenter.

102. In verbs of the 3rd conjugation which end in ඉ, the final consonant of the root is doubled before ව and the final vowel ඉ is changed into අ, Ex; අදිනවා to drag, අද්දවනවා, cause to be dragged.

103. If the final ඉ of the root is incorporated with the cerebral letter ර, ළ, ට, or ඩ, the consonant is not generally reduplicated, but the final vowel ඉ is changed into අ.

EXAMPLES. උදාහරණ.

අරිනවා	to send	අරවනවා.
සිටිනවා	to stand	සිටවනවා.

104. If the final ඉ of the root is incorporated with the conjunct letter ඟ, ඳ or ඹ, the seminasal is separated and written in full.

EXAMPLES. උදාහරණ.

නඟිනවා	to ascend,	නංගවනවා.
බඳිනවා	to bind	බන්දවනවා.
පිඹිනවා	to blow,	පිම්බවනවා.

105. The final ස් or හ් of the root is reduplicated before ව even if it is not incorporated with ඉ Ex:—ගසනවා to beat, ගස්සවනවා.

106. The letter හ් when reduplicated assumes the form ස්. Ex:—වහනවා to cover, වස්සවනවා.

Exception—The causal form of බොනවා, to drink, is පොවනවා.

107. In forming the causal past the final vowel of the root is changed into එ.
Ex; කඩනවා break, කැඩෙව්වා, caused to be broken.

Note:—The process of the formation of the past tense its explained in Lesson 11.

EXERCISE XXI. 21 අභ්‍යාස පාඩම.

(a.) Give the causal forms present and past of the following verbs:—

කියනවා, to say; දෙනවා, to give; වඳිනවා, to worship; අඳිනවා, to dress; වහනවා, to cover; පනිනවා, to jump; සූර නවා, to scrape; ගිලිනවා, to swallow; පිහිනවා, to sweep;

නඟිනවා, to ascend; අනිනවා, to butt, to hit; පිඹිනවා, to blow; නිදහස්කරනවා, to release; බිඳිනවා, to break; ඉරනවා, to tear, to saw; තල්ලුකරනවා, to shove; පදිනවා, to row; අතුරනවා, to spread; ඔබනවා, to press down; බානවා, to let down; පුලුස්සනවා to burn, සරසනවා to decorate,

(b.) Translate the following:--

මගේ පියා වැඩකාරයන් ලවා වත්තේ වැට බන්දවනවා. මේ මිනිහා මට බැන්නෙවුවා. අද මම තට ගස්සවනවා. අපි හරකුන් ලවා හෙට කුඹුර හාවනවා. මගේ වත්තේ ඉනි කැප්පෙවුවේ කවුද? මම අද සවස ගෙදරට පිදුරු අද්දවනවා. හරකුන්ට වතුර පොවාපන්. මම ඒ මිනිහා ලවා මගේ ගේ සාදවන්ට ඕනෑ. මහත්මයා කුලීකාරයන් ලවා පාර සාදවනවා. මම කොල්ලන් ලවා ඔරුව පද්දවාගන ගඟෙන් එගොඩ උනා. අද උදේ මම මගේ ගස්වල පොල් කැඩෙව්වා. මාමා ලමයින් සෙකෝලයට නොයවන්නේ මන්ද? මම ඉඩමක මිණිරන් හාරවනවා. මේ මිනිහා දිවුරවපන්.

I got the tree cut by the servant. Feed this child. Make him to do the work. I caused the thief to be seized. Who got him to write the letter? He got a well sunk (dug) in the garden. I got him to swear. Have this letter sent to the post office. Who asked you to send the servant to the boutique? Some one caused my money to be stolen by my servants. This man caused my house to be burnt

---

LESSON XXII. 22 පාඩම.

30. THE CONDITIONAL MOOD.

108. The conditional mood is formed by affixing නත් or තොත් to the base of the present tense and අත් or ඔත් to that of the past tense. නම්, if subjoined to a finite verb, has the same force as තොත් or ඔත්.

EXAMPLES. උදාහරණ.

මරතත් බොරු නොකියන්, though you be killed do not tell lies.

උඹ යකොත් මම නවතිනවා, if you go I (shall) remain

ඔහු ගියත් කාරණයක් නොවෙයි, it does not matter even if he went

වැස්සොත් මම කුඹුර හානවා, if it rains I (shall plough the field.

109. The suffixesද්දී added to the base of the present tense and අම to that of the past tense express the time when.

EXAMPLES. උදාහරණ.

බල්ලා බුරද්දී හොරු දිව්වා, when the dog was barking the thieves ran (away)

ඉර බැස්සාම අපි පිටත්වෙනවා, when the sun has set we (shall) start.

31. THE OPTATIVE

110. The optative is foromed by affixing වා to verbs of the present tense, after the terminations indicating persons.

EXAMPLES. උදාහරණ.

ඔහු රජ වේවා may he become king

ඔහු මට පෙනේවා, may he appear to me

32. PERMISSIVE FORM.

The permissive form of the verb is formed by adding ආවේ to the past paticipial adjective

EXAMPLES. උදාහරණ.

ගියාවේ. let him go; මැරුනාවේ, let him die; ආවාවේ, let him come; සිටපුවාවේ let him stay.

Note:—The first ව in ආවාවේ and සිටපුවාවේ is an augmentation (ආගම.) ආ+ආවේ=ආවාවේ.

EXERCISE XXII. 22 අභ්‍යාස පාඩම.

Translate the following:—

වශ්‍රාව වැස්සොත් මම කුඹුරහානවා. ඉර බසිද්දි ලමයි ගෙදර ආවා. උඹ ගමට යතොත් මම උඹේ පඩි දෙන්නේ නෑ. උඹ ඇත්ත කියතත් මහත්මයා ඒක විශ්වාස කරන්නේ නෑ. උඹ ගෙදර යනවානම් මගේ ලමයා සමග පලයන්. ගමට ගියාම අපි මහත්මයාට වැඩකාරණයක් එවනවා. මගේ සතුරු මැරේවා. උඹට හොඳක් වේවා. අපට මුදල් ලැබේවා. මට රුපියල් දෙකක් දුන්නොත් මම ඒ වැඩේ කරනවා. කුලි දෙතත් මම තමුසේගේ වැඩේ කරන්නේ නෑ. කොල්ලා ගමට ගියාවේ. බල්ලා පීනුවාවේ.

If he runs he will catch the thief. Although I be beaten I will not do the work. When he was going along the road the thief took his comb. After the sun set the boys came home. Whilst the dogs were barking the thieves entered the house. May my friend become rich. May your enemy perish. Let the servant cut the tree. Let the dog eat his food.

LESSON XXIII. 23 පාඩම.

32. Inflectional Terminations of Verbs.

111. In colloquial Sinhalese, as shown in the preceding lessons, the same form of a vowel is used for the three persons, singular and plural, in the present, past, and future tenses of the Indicative Mood. There are, however, in strict grammar, special terminations for each person, singular and plural. These are given below.

Indicative Mood. Active Voice.

Present Tense.

Singular.	Plural.
1. මි, එමි	1. මු, එමු, මිහ
2. එහි, හි	2. හු
3. ඉ, ඒ	3. අත්, ඉත්, එත්, ඃති, ඉති, එති.

Past Tense.

Singular.	Plural.
1. එමි, එම්, ඉමි	1. එමු, මිහ, මු, මෝ
2. එහි,	2. හු
3. ඊ, ඒ, අ	3. ඕ, හු, හ

Future Tense.

Singular.	Plural.
1. අන්නෙමි	1. අන්නෙමු
2. අන්නෙහි	2. අන්නාහු
3. අන්නේ	3. අන්නෝ

34. Paradigms of Conjugation.

Root මර--මරනවා, to kill.

Active Voice. Indicative Mood.

Present Tense.

Singular.		Plural.	
1. මරමි,	I kill	1. මරමු,	we kill
2. මරහි,	thou killest	2. මරහු,	you kill
3. මරයි,	he kills	3. මරති, මරත්,	they kill

Past Tense.

Singular.		Plural.	
1. මැරුවෙමි, මැරීමි,	I killed	1. මැරුවෙමු, මැරීමු,	we killed
2. මැරුවෙහි, මැරීහි,	thou killedst	2. මැරුවහු, මැරීහු,	you killed
3. මැරුවේ, මැරී,	he killed	3. මැරුවෝ, මැරීහ,	they killed

Future Tense.

Singular.		Plural.	
1. මරන්නෙමි,	I shall kill	2. මරන්නෙමු,	we shall kill
2. මරන්නෙහි,	thou shalt kill	2. මරන්නහු,	you shall kill
3. මරන්නේ,	he will kill	3. මරන්නෝය,	they will kill

Optative Mood.

Singular.		Plural.	
1. මැරෙම්වා,	may I die	1. මැරෙමුවා,	may we die
2. මැරෙහිවා,	mayest thou die	2. මැරෙහුවා,	may you die
3. මැරේවා,	may he die	3. මැරෙත්වා,	may they die

Instransitive Verb.

මැරෙනවා. to die.

Indicative Mood.

Present Tense.

Singular.		Plural.	
1. මැරෙමි,	I die	1. මැරෙමු, මැරෙම්හ,	we die
2. මැරෙහි,	thou diest	2. මැරෙහු,	you die
3. මැරේ, මැරෙයි,	he dies	3. මැරෙත්, මැරෙති	they die

Past Tense.

Singular.		Plural.	
1. මැරුණෙමි,	I died	1. මැරුණෙමු,	we died
2. මැරුණෙහි,	thou diedst	2. මැරුණහු,	you died
3. මැරුණේ,	he died	3. මැරුණෝ,	they died

Future Tense.

Singular.		Plural.	
1. මැරෙන්නෙමි,	I shall die	1. මැරෙන්නෙමු,	we shall die
2. මැරෙන්නෙහි,	thou shalt die	2. මැරෙන්නහු,	you shall die
3. මැරෙන්නේ,	he will die	3. මැරෙන්නෝය,	they shall die

CAUSAL FORM.

ACTIVE VOICE. INDICATIVE MOOD.

Present Tense.

Singular.	Plural.
1. මරවමි	1. මරවමු
2. මරවහි	2. මරවහු
3. මරවයි	3. මරවත්

Past Tense.

Singular.	Plural
1. මැරෙවූවෙම්	1. මැරෙවූවෙමි
2. මැරෙවූවෙහි	2. මැරෙවූවහු
3. මැරෙවූවේ	3. මැරෙවූවෝ

Future Tense.

Singular.	Plural.
1. මරවන්නෙමි	1. මරවන්නෙමු
2. මරවන්නෙහි	2. මරවන්නාහු
3. මරවන්නේ	3. මරවන්නෝ

PASSIVE VOICE. INDICATIVE MOOD.

Present Tense.

Singular.	Plural
1. මරනුලබමි, I am killed	1. මරනුලබමු, we are killed
2. මරනුලබහි thou art killed	2. මරනුලබහු, you are killed
3 මරනුලබයි, he is killed	3. මරනුලබත්, they are killed

Past Tense.

Singular.

1.	මරන ලද්දෙමි,	මරනු ලැබුවෙමි,	I was killed
2.	මරන ලද්දෙහි,	මරනු ලැබුවෙහි,	thou wast killed
3.	මරන ලද්දේ,	මරනු ලැබුවේ,	he was killed

Plural.

1. මරන ලද්දෙමු, මරනු ලැබුවෙමු, we were killed
2. මරන ලද්දෙහි, මරනු ලැබුවහු, you were killed
3. මරන ලද්දෝ, මරනු ලැබුවෝ they were killed

Future Tense.

Singular.

1. මරනු ලබන්නෙමි, I shall be killed
2. මරනු ලබන්නෙහි, thou shalt be killed
3. මරනු ලබන්නේ, he will be killed

Plural.

1. මරනු ලබන්නෙමු, we shall be killed
2. මරනු ලබන්නාහු, you shalt be killed
3. මරනු ලබන්නෝ, they will be killed

EXERCISE XXIII. 23. අභ්‍යාස පාඩම.

Translate the following:—

දූන් මම කන්තෝරුවට යමි. තෝ ගමේ නාත්තෙහිද? බල්ලෝ හොරුන්ට බුරත්. උඹේ මස්සිනා හොරා අල්ලයි. බල්ලන් විසින් ඌරු මරනලද්දේ (ය). ගොවියා විසින් කුඹුර හානු ලැබේ. හෙට මම වත්තේ වැට බඳින්නෙමි. රදවා රෙදි සෝදයි. දෙන්නු කිරි දෙත්. බළලා විසින් මීයෙක් මරනලද්දේය. මම ඒ වැඩේ කරන්නෙමි. අපි ගස් කැපූවෙමු. උඹ කපාලා තිබුණු ගහ මා විසින් අද්දවනලද්දේය. උඹේ බඩු ගත් සොරු අපි ඇල්ලූවෙමු. හරක් කැලේට දුවත්. උඹලා කුඹුර හැවගුද? වැඩකාරයන් ලවා මම හෙට වත්තේ වැට බන්දවමි. මේ මිනිහා අපේ ගේ පිළිස්සෙවුවේය. අපේ ගමේ ලෙඩදුක් නැතිවේවා. හොරු නැතිවෙත්වා. උඹ ලමයින් අඬවන්නෙහිද?

Translate the following sentences into Sinhalese:—

The elephants bathe in the tank. The boatmen will row the boat across the river. I snatched the knife from the thief. They drink toddy. We burried the dead cow. Was the man sworn? Get the boy to do the work. I killed the bird These trees grow well. My horse runs fast. The sun shines to-day. The compound was swept by the servant woman. May the sun shine. You gave me the cow. The goat was killed by the leopard. I dig a pit. The tree falls,

---

LESSON XXIV. 24 පාඩම.

35. Compounds. සමාස.

112. A Samasa is a compound of two or more words, as අත් පොත, hand book (අත් hand and පොත book.)

Compounds are divided into five classes, viz.

(1) අවියසමස් or අව්‍යය සමාස, indeclinable compounds
(2) විබත් සමස් or විභක්ති සමාස, case compounds
(3) වෙසෙසුන් සමස් or විශෙෂණ සමාස, adjectival compounds
(4) අන්අරුත් සමස් or අන්‍යාර්ථ සමාස, relative compounds
(5) දඅරුත් සමස් or ද්වාර්ථ සමාස, collective compounds.

Indeclinable ompounds.

113. An indeclinable compound is formed by prefixing an indeclinable particle to another word.

Examples. උදාහරණ.

දුදන,	bad man;	(දු bad	+	දන	man)
සුවඳ,	good smell;	(සු good	+	ගඳ	smell,)
අසරණ,	helpless;	(අ not	+	සරණ	help.)
අකුසල්,	sin;	(අ not	+	කුසල්	merit.)

2. Case Compounds

114. A case compound is formed of two nouns of which the first is in its crude form,

Examples. උදාහරණ.

වැඩකරු, servant; (work doer) [Acc. case]
පරපුටු, beggar, cuckoo; (nourished by stranger) [Inst. case]
ලීබඩු, furniture, (things made with wood) [Aux. case]
ලෝකාඵ, public good, (benefit for the world) Dat. case]
සොරබිය, fear arisiug from thieves; [Ab. case]
හරක්මස්, beef; (flesh of the ox) [Gen. case]
නගරවාසි, citizen; (dweller in the city) [Loc. case]

3. Adjectival Compounds.

115. An adjectival compound is a compound formed of an adjective and a noun, නිලුපුල්, blue lotns, (නිල් blue + උපුල් lotous), තුන්ලෝ, the three worlds, (තුන් three + ලෝ worlds).

4. Relative Compounds.

116. A Relative Compound bears a signification different from that conveyed by its component parts.

Examples. උදාහරණ.

ශතපත්‍ර, lotus, (ශත hundred + පත්‍ර leaves)
බස්නාහිර, west, (බස්නා descending + හිර sun)

(5) Collective Compounds.

A compound formed by the combination of two nouns in their crude state without a connecting particle is called a collective Compound.

Examples. උදාහරණ.

හිරසඳ, sun and moon
අත්පා, hand and foot

Vocabulary 7.

අක්කරය, acre
සේරුව, measure, $\frac{1}{32}$ part of a bushel
කුරුණිය, $\frac{1}{8}$ of a bushel
පැල, measure equal to ten kurunis
අමුණ, measure equal to 5 bushels. Superficial measure containing as much ground as an amunam of grain will sow.
නැළිය, $\frac{1}{32}$ part of a bushel,
ලාහ, measure of quantity equal to 4 nelis

ගොයම,	corn	මෝසම,	harvest time
යල,	one of the harvests	මහ,	one of the harvests
නගුල,	plough	නියර,	ridge, dam
ගොවියා,	cultivator	ගොවිතැන,	cultivation
හිස් ඉඩම,	waste land	හේන,	chena land
පංගුව, කොටස,	share	බිත්තරවී,	seed paddy
අස්වැන්න,	crops	පිදුරු,	straw
බාන,	pair,	මීහරකා,	buffalo

එළහරක්, cattle in contradistinction to buffaloes
ප්‍රමාණය, extent — ලියැද්ද, division of a paddy field

EXCERCISE XXIV. 24 අභ්‍යාස පාඩම.

Name the class of compound to which each of the following belongs.

වීගොවිතැන, paddy cultivation; වපසරිය, sowing extent; ගංවතුර, river water; සහෝදරයෝ, brothers; මව්පියෝ, parents; වැසි හුළං, rain and wind; මහ වැව, big tank; අනදර, injustice; නැගෙනහිර, east; සිව්පාවෝ, quadrupeds; රා අරක්කු, toddy and arrack, උණුවතුර, hot water; සීල්වතුර (සිසිල් වතුර), cold water; මඩ බිම, mud land; බදු ඔප්පුව, lease; පොල් තෙල්, cocoanut oil; ගංතෙර, river bank; හිස්ඉඩම්, waste lands; තණබිම, grass lands; කුරුඳුවතු, cinnamon lands; පංගුකාරයෝ, share holders; බිම්කට්ටිය, portion of land.

Translate the following:—

(a.) මගේ කුඹුරේ වී දෙපැලක් වැපුරුණා. යල් මෝසමට ඉඩම් වැඩකරන්නේ මේ මාසේදීය. මගේ පොල්වත්ත මී හරකුන් ලවා හාවන්ට ඕනෑ. මේ අවුරුද්දේ අස්වැන්න අඩුයි. මම අක්කර පහක මුඩුබිමක් මිලේට ගත්තෙමි. මම වැපුරුවේ වී දෙපැලයි. උඹේ ගොයම කපන්නේ කවදාද? මා විසින් මිලේටගත් ඉඩමේ ප්‍රමාණය අක්කර විස්සයි. මට තෑගි දුන් ඉඩම පහලොස් අමුනයි. මම වැපිරීමට බිත්තර වී තුන්ලහක් ණයට ගත්තා. උඹේ කුඹුරේ නියර උඩින් මිනිහෙකුටවත් යන්ට බෑ. ඉඩමේ පංගුකාරයෝ පස්දෙනෙකි. මගේ ලියැද්ද ලී නගුලකින් හාන්ට බෑ හෙට මගේ කුඹුර හාන්ට ගොන් බානක් ඕනෑකරනවා. මම හරක් බානක් ගොවියෙකුට වික්කෙමි. බිත්තර වී කුරුණි පහක් මම උඹට දෙන්නෙමි.

(b.) Who are the shareholders? What is the sowing extent of your field? I brought from the village sixty bundles of straw. I had good crops this year. There are no chena lands in this village. October is the sowing month for the maha harvest. Poor people make their ploughs of wood. A pela of paddy is equal to ten kurunis. People of this village are all cultivators. September is the reaping month of the yala harvest. I bought all the shares of this land. I must construct a dam to the west of my field.

LESSON XXV. 25 පාඩම.

36. Prefixes. උපසර්ග.

Upasarga are indeclinable particles prefixed to nouns, verbs &c. Words when compounded with these prefixes sometimes retain the meaning of the original, but in many instances they effect certain modifications in the ideas conveyed. These prefixes are about twenty in number and are given below, with their significations examplified by words compounded with prefixes.

Prefixes.	Signification.	Examples.	
අති,	beyond	ඉතුරු,	exceeding
අදි,	over	අදියර,	chapter
අනු,	after	අනුබල,	support
අප,	off	අපදන්,	taking away
අබි,	opposite	අබිදම්,	metaphysics
අව,	off	අවසන්,	conclusion
අ, අප,	reversing	අගම්,	augmentation
උ,	on	උගනී,	he learns
උප,	near	උවම්, උපමා,	simile
දු,	bad	දුදන,	wicked men
නි,	without	නිදොස්,	without fault
පර,	back	පැරදුම,	defeat
පිරි,	around	පිරිවර,	retinue
ප,	out, very	පසිඳු,	famous
පිළි,	again	පිළිතුරු,	reply
වි,	apart	විබත්,	case
ස,	with	සබඳ,	connected
සු,	well	සුදන,	good men

Sanskrit Equivalents.

Prefixes.	Signification.	Examples.	
අති,	beyond	අතිරික්ත,	exceeding
අධි,	over,	අධිගත,	gone over.
අනු,	after	අනුචර,	attendant.
අප,	off	අපහෘත,	taking off.
අභි,	opposite	අභිමුඛ,	preseuce.
අව,	off	අවසාන,	conclusion.
ආ,	reversing	ආගමන,	coming
උද්,	on	උද්ග්‍රහණ,	learning.
උප,	near	උපවන,	neighbouring
දුඃ*	bad	දුර්ගන්ධ,	bad smell, [forest.
නිඃ, †	without	නිර්දෝෂ,	without fault.

* Changed into දුර්, දුශ්, දුෂ්, දුස්.

† Changed into නිර්, නිශ්, නිෂ්, නිස්.

පරා,	back	පරාජය,	defeat
පරි,	around	පරිපූර්ණ,	perfect
ප්‍ර,	out, forward	ප්‍රශ්වාස,	expirated breath
ප්‍රති,	again	ප්‍රත්‍යුත්තර,	reply
වි,	apart	වියෝග,	disunion
සං,	with	සම්බන්ධ,	connected
සු,	well	සුගන්ධ,	good smell

EXERCISE XXV. අභ්‍යාස පාඩම.

Point out the prefixes in the following words :—

පිළිපදිනවා, observe ; **පවර,** great ; **දුබල,** powerless ; **දුසිරිත්,** vice ; **සුවඳ,** good smell ; **අනුමත,** consent ; **නිර්මල,** without blemish ; **නිශ්ශබ්ද,** silence ; **නිරන්තර,** always ; **විපත,** calamity ; **දුශ්චරිත,** vice ; **ආශ්වාස,** inhaled air ; **සංගම,** association ; **උපඒජන්ත,** Assistant Agent ; **සුදුසු,** fit ; **ප්‍රමාණ,** extent ; **විලාසය,** form; **සසර,** metempsychosis; **උමග,** tunnel ; **නිෂ්ඵල,** fruitless ; useless ; **පිළිගන්නවා,** accept ; **උපලේඛනය,** schedule, appendix ; **සම්පූර්ණ,** perfect ; **උපක්‍රමය,** means ; **නිවැරදි,** guiltless ; **අවනම්බු,** dishonour ; **අධිපතියා,** chief person ; **ආඥාව,** order ; **ආඥාපණත,** ordinance ; **ගමනාගමන,** passing and repassing.

Translate the following :-

මම ඒ තෑග්ග පිළිගත්තේ නෑ. මේ උපක්‍රමයෙන් හොරු ගෙට ඇතුල්උනා. සූදුකෙළිය අවනම්බුවට කාරණයකි. උපඒජන්තතුමාගේ ආඥාව පිළිපදින්ට'ඕනෑ. වැඩකාරයා ගමට ගොස් සම්පූර්ණයෙන් මාසයක් පසුඋණා. ඒ ආඥාපණතේ උපලේඛනය බලනු. කඩුගන්නාවේ උමග බොහෝදිගයි. මිනිහෙක් මිනිත්තුවකට 18 වාරයක් පමණ ආශ්වාස ප්‍රශ්වාස කරනවා. මගේ ගමන නිෂ්ඵල උනා. මම ගමේ අධිපතියා ළඟට ගියා. උඹේ ඉඩමේ ප්‍රමාණය උඹ දන්නේ නැද්ද? මේ කාලේ දැනට සූදුකෙළිය රා අරක්කු බීම ආදි දුශ්චරිත පවතිනවා. මට ලොකු විපත්තියක් පැමුණුණා. මගේ පියා දුබල අයෙකි.

ඊයේ අපේ ගමේ ලොකු සංගමයක් පැවැත්තුවා. මේ පාරේ ගමනාගමනයකරන්නෝ බොහෝ වෙති. මගේ මස්සිනා නඩුවෙන් නිවැරදිකාරයා උනා. මමත් නිවැරදිකාරයෙකි. ගමේ මුලාදෑනියා හොරුන්ට අනුබල දෙනවා.

LESSON XXVI. 26. පාඩම.

37. ADVERBS ක්‍රියා විශෙෂණ.

119. The adverb generally comes before the word which it modifies, as is ඔහු ඉක්මනින් දිව්වා, he ran quickly. The particles ලෙස, as ; සේ, as; කොට having done ; ව, having become ; ට, ඉන්, and එන්, are affixed to nouns and adjectives to form adverbs.

EXAMPLS. උදාහරණ.

සුදුසු,	proper	සුදුසු ලෙස,	properly
මනා,	good	මනාසේ,	well
යහපත්,	good	යහපත්කොට	well
මනා,	good	මනාව,	well
හොඳ,	good	හොඳට,	well
දුක,	grief	දුකින්,	with grief
සැප,	comfort	සැපෙන්,	comfortably

120. The adverbs කල්, untill; තුරු, until; තෙක්, as long as; විට, when; කොට, when; are used after verbal adjectives present.

EXAMPLES. උදාහරණ.

ඉර බසින කල්, until the sun sets
මා එන තුරු, untill I come
මා ජීවත්ව සිටින තෙක්, as long as I live
උඹ කතා කරනවිට, when you speak
මිනිහා වැටෙනකොට, when the man falls

121. Ordinal numeral adjectives may be turned into adverbs by suffixing ව, as in පළමුවෙනුව, firstly; දෙවනුව, secondly; තුන්වෙනුව, thirdly.

122. The following list of adverbs and those given in Vocabulary 5 may be commited to memory.

Vocabulary 7.

Adverbs of time.

අතරතුර, during
අනිද්දා, day after to-morrow
ඉන්අනිද්දා, three days hence
ඉස්සර, of old, before
එතකල්, until then
එතකොට, then
එදා, that day
කඩිනමට, soon
කලාතුරකින්, seldom
දැනට, for the present
දෙවනු, afterwards
නැවත, again
නිතර, always
නොකඩව, } continuously, regularly
පළමුදා, the third day back
පසුව, පස්සේ, } afterwards
පෙරෙයිදා, the day before yesterday
බාගවෙලාවට, sometimes
මත්තට, in the future
මෑතදී, lately
මින්මතු, hereafter
මෙලහකට, by this time
රෑට, to-night
ළඟදී, lately
වරින්වර, කලින්කල, } from time to time
වහාම, forthwith
විටින්විට, from time to time.
වේලාසනින්, early
සමහරවිට, sometimes
සෑමදාම, every day
දවස්පතා, daily

Adverbs of place.

අතන, there
ඈත, afar
ඉදිරිපිට. before
ඉහළ, above
එතන, there
ඔබ, yonder
ඔබමොබ, here and there
ඉස්සරහ, in front
ඉවත, aside
උඩ, above
මෙතන, here
යට, under
ළඟට, near
වටේට, around

තැනින්තැන, from place to place
පිට, out
මෙන්න, here
හරහට, across
හාත්පසින්, on all sides

ADVERBS OF MANNER &c.

ඇත්තටම, truly
ඉතාම, very
ඉබේම } by chance
ඉබේට }
ඉන්නිසා therefore
එහෙම, in that manner
ඒ නිසා, therefore
එපමණ, that much
ඔපමණ, so much
කොහොමවත්, any how
කොහෙත්ම, at all
තදේට } strongly
තදින් }
තනියම, alone
තව } more
තවත් }
දඩාවතේ, astray
නැවතිල්ලේ, slowly
නිකම්, without work
බලෙන් } by force
බලේට }
බොහෝවිට, frequently
බොහෝකොට, greatly
මදක්, a little
යන්තම්, narrowly
වැඩිය, more
වැරෙන්, } strongly
වැරේට, }
වැඩිපුර, over and above
වෙනම, separately
සැබෑවට, truly
සත්තකට, truly, surely
හොරෙන්, stealthily
හෙමින්, slowly
යහමින්, abundantly

EXERCISE XXVI. 26. අභ්‍යාස පාඩම.

Translate the following:—

(a.) මේ වත්තේ කුරුඳු හොඳට වැවෙනවා. උඹේ වැඩකාරයා නිතරම එතන මෙතන ඇවිදින්නේ මන්ද? අපි මෙහි සැපසේ ජීවත්වෙනවා. මිනිහා රදවාට ගහනකොට මගේ අය්යා එතන හිටියේ නැහැ. ඉර බසිනතුරු මම වෙලේ සිටියා. පෙරෙයිදා හොරු දෙදෙනෙක් අපේ ඔරුව හොරකම් කරගෙන යන්ට උත්සාහ කළා. ළමයිනි උඹලා දවස්පතා නාන්ට ඕනෑ. ඔහු මේ ගෙදරට ඇවිත් දැනට අවුරුද්දක් වෙනවා. මේ මිනිහා රෑ බිබී එතන මෙතන ඇවිදිනවා. අපේ කුඹුරට ගංවතුර ගලන්නේ කලාතුරකිනි. අවුරුදු දහයකට

ඉස්සර මේ පාර ගංවතුරට යටවුනා. මේ ඔය හරහට පාලමක් දැම්මොත් හොඳයි. අපේ ගමේ මූකලානට කලින්කල කොටි ඇවිත් වදිනවා.

(b.) I must plough my field the day after to-morrow. I brought him here by force. I was there alone until sun set. He was sowing paddy when I went. Walk slowly. You took away my dog stealthily. It rained abundantly last night. Yesterday my cows went stray. You must do this work any how. Surely I did not tell you to go. I received that much. This man gets intoxicated frequently. I shall be here until you write the letter.

LESSON XXVII. 27. පාඩම.

CONJUNCTIONS.

123. Conjunctions consisting of one letter are generally affixed to words, as in උඹද මමද you and I; උඹ හෝ මම හෝ, you or I; උඹත් මමත්, you and I.

124. The following list of conjunctions may be commited to memory.

Vocabulary 8.

ද, and
ත්, and
හෝ, or
සහ, and, with
හා and, with
වත්, or
තවද, moreover
හෙවත්, alias
නොහොත්, or
එක්කෝ, or
ඇරත්, besides
එහෙත්, but
නුමුත්, but
ඉතින්, and then, after that
ඉන්නිසා, therefore
එබැවින්, therefore
හරි, or
නැත්නම්, if not

125. The conjunctions ද, ත්, හෝ, and වත් are used after each of the words, joined as in the examples given above.

126. The word preceding සහ or හා should be in the instrumental case as in බල්ලන් සහ කුකුළෝ, the dogs and the fowls or the fowls with dogs.

127. When ත් is used after a noun ending in a mute consonant, the vowel උ is inserted between ත් and the mute consonant, as in කොල්ලෙකුත්, හරකුත්, a boy and oxen.

EXERCISE XXVII. 27. අභ්‍යාස පාඩම.

Translate the following:—

ඔහුත් මමත් අනිද්දා රත්නපුරයට යනවා. එළුවන් සහ ඌරෝ නිතරම මේ ගෙදරට එනවා. මගේ මාමා මේ ගෙදරට කවදාවත් ආවේවත් මා සමග කථාකළේවත් නෑ. ඔහු එතනට ගියේවත් නෑ. හිරගෙයින් සැඟවී ගිය මිනිහාගේ නම කරෝලිස් හෙවත් කරෝ අප්පුය. උඹ නොහොත් උඹේ මස්සිනා මගේ ගස්වල පුවක් සොරකම්කළා. උඹ එක්කෝ උඹේ මලයා මේ වැට බඳින්ට ඕනෑ. උඹ අද මගේ මුදල දෙන්ට ඕනෑ. නැත්නම් මම උඹට විරුඩව පැමිනිල්ලක් ගන්නවා. මගේ පියාද මවද සහෝදරයෝද පල්ලියට ගියා. උඹ හෝ උඹේ යාළුවා හෝ වැඩේ කරන්ට ඕනෑ. ඒ මිනිහා, මගේ පුතාට ඊයේ බැන්නා. ඒ නිසා මම අද ඔහුට ගැහුවා.

You or I must go to Kandy. The dog and the bears came out of the jungle. Ebony and Satin are found in abundance in that district. I will cut your fence or ridge. I sold my land called Koswatta alias Miwatta. Either he or his brother must pay the money. I gave him the book, but he did not pay for it. My children go to school regularly, but they do not learn their lessons well.

LESSON XXVIII. 28. පාඩම.

39. INTERJECTIONS.

අඃ, tut! (expressing disappointment)

අපොයි
අනේ
අයියෝ
අහෝ
අනිච්චත් } Alas! (expressing grief or pain)

ඉලව්වේ
උලව්වේ } death! (expressing horror)

චී,
චී චී,
චීඃ } pshaw! expressing contempt)

බොල
බොලන්
අඩේ
අඩෝ
අඩී (fem)
ඕයි
ඒයි } used in addressing another

Vocabulary 9.

මාසය, month
ජනවාරි, January
පෙබරවාරි, February
මාර්තු, March
අප්‍රියෙල්, April
මැයි, May
ජුනි, June
ජුලි, July
අගෝස්තු, August
සැප්තැම්බර්, September
ඔක්තෝබර්, October
නොවැම්බර්, November
දෙසැම්බර්, December
දවස, දා, දින, day

ඉරිදා, Sunday
සඳුදා, Monday
අඟහරුවාදා, Tuesday
බදාදා, Wednesday
බ්‍රහස්පතින්දා, Thursday
සිකුරාදා, Friday
සෙනසුරාදා, Saturday
සතිය, සුමානය, week
පැය, hour
මිනිත්තුව, minute
මොහොත, moment
පසළොස්වක, full moon
අමාවක, new moon
අටවක, the 8th day after the new or full moon
පෝය, quarters of the moon

Sinhalese months	Nearly corresponding to
බක්	April
වෙසක්	May
පොසොම්	June
ඇසළ	July
නිකිණි	August
බිණර	September
වප්, වක්	October
ඉල්,	November
උඳුවප්, උඳුවක්	December
දුරුතු	January
නවම්	Eebruary
මැදින්දින,	March

Note:—බක් begins about the 12th of April and මැදින් දින ends about the 11th of March.

EXERCISE XXVIII. අහතස පාඩම.

Translate the following:—

(a.) අපොයි මගේ හිස කකියනවා. වෙසක් මාසේ පසළොස්වක හෙටයි. අනේ මහත්මයා මට සඳුදාට ගමට යන්ට අවසර දෙන්ට ඕනෑ. මැයි මාසේ බොහොම වැසි වසිනවා. අනිච්චන් මේ ගිගන්නාගේ කාසි හොරෙක් උදුරාගෙන තිබෙනවා. ගිය සෙනසුරාදා පෝය දවසකි. මේ අවුරුද්දේ වෙසක් පසළොස්වක වැටෙන්නේ මැයි මාසේ දහඅටවෙනි බදාදාටයි. ච් ච් ළමයා අරක්කු බොන්ට එපා. බොලන් ඉස්සීනෙ උඹ ඔය මිනිහාගේ කීම අහලා රැවටෙන්ට එපා. අඃ මට ඒක ගෙනෙන්ට මතකනැතිවුනා. වප් මාසේදී අපේ කුඹුරේ වී වැපුරුවා. සිංහල අලුත් අවුරුද්ද වැටෙන්නේ බොහෝ කොට අප්‍රියෙල් මාසේ එකොළොස් වෙනිදාටයි අඩේ මෙගෙ වර.

(b.) I purchased the land on Monday the 25th of last month. There was much rain on Tuesday and Wednesday. I was there about 3 hours on Sunday. Pshaw! dont drink toddy. Alas! he died very young. November is generally a rainy month. Wap is the sowing month. He was three weeks in the town. Bak is the first month of the Sinhalese year. Buddha was born on the full moon day in the month of Wesak.

LESSON XXIX. 29 පාඩම.

AUXILIARY VERBS.

40. කරනවා to do, වෙනවා to become.

128. By suffixing කරනවා and වෙනවා, to certain stems of nouns, adjectives, or indeclinable words, new verbs are formed. Those which are in common use are given below.

Vocabulary 10.

ඇතුල්කරනවා, to put in	ඇතුල්වෙනවා, to get in
අච්චුකරනවා, to punish	සම්බවෙනවා, to meet
කඩකරනවා, to violate	යාවෙනවා, to be adjoined
තල්ලුකරනවා, to shove	සුවවෙනවා, to be cured
සම්බකරනවා, to earn	දියවෙනවා, to be dissolved
යාකරනවා, to connect	භයවෙනවා, to be frightened
විසිකරනවා, to throw	නැතිවෙනවා, to be lost
ඉෂ්ටකරනවා, to accomplish	විසිවෙනවා, to be thrown
වියදම්කරනවා, to spend	අහුවෙනවා, to be caught
නරක්කරනවා, to spoil	නරක්වෙනවා, to be spoilt
සණ්ඩුකරනවා, to quarrel	පත්තුවෙනවා, to be burnt
ඕනෑකරනවා, to require	මාරුවෙනවා, to be dismissed
එපාකරනවා, to reject, to refuse	කළුවෙනවා, to be blackened
නැත්කරනවා, to ruin, to lose	වියදම්වෙනවා, to be spent
ඇතිකරනවා, to bring up, to rear	සිද්ධවෙනවා, to take place

EXERCISE XXIX. 29 අභ්‍යාස පාඩම.

Translate the following :—

(a) උඹේ පුතා මගේ වත්තට හරකුන් ඇතුල්කළා නොවේද? උඹේ වත්තට කව්රුවත් හරකුන් ඇතුල් කළේ නෑ. නුමුත් වත්තේ වැටක් නැති නිසා හරක් ඇතුල්වුනා. උඹ ඊගියේ වීසිකළාම ලමයි භයවෙලා ගෙදර දිව්වා. මගේ කුඹුරත් ඒ මිනිහාගේ කුඹුරට යාවෙන නුමුත් වෙන වෙන නම් ඇති ඉඩම් දෙකකි. මේ පළාතේ මිනිස්සු බුඩාගම්කාරයෝ නුමුත් රා අරක්කු බොනවා, ඌරන් කුකුළන් ඇතිකරනවා. ඒ මිනිස්සු ගෙනා පොල්පැණි නරක්වෙලා තිබුණු නිසා මම ඒවා එපා කළා. මගේ පුතා ගිය අව්රුද්දේ සම්බකළ කාසි සියල්ලම කැමබීමට වියදම් උනා. සොරකමින් සම්බකරන කාසි ඉක්මනින් නැතිවෙනවා. මගේ පරණ සපත්තුකුට්ටම කළුකරලා කාමරේට ගෙනත් දියන්. මේ ගෙවල් දෙකේ ඉන්න මිනිස්සු නිතරම සණ්ඩුකරනවා. තමුන්නාන්සේගේ වැඩකාරයා මාව තල්ලුකළ නිසා මම ඌට පාරක් ගැහුවා. ඒ වේලාවට පාර අද්දර ගෙවල්වල පාන් පත්තුඋනා. ඌ උගේ ගෙදර පාන පත්තුකළේ කොයි වේලාවේද? අතිසාර රෝගේ වැළඳී සිටි තමුසේගේ බෑනා සුවකළේ කව්ද? ඒ ලමයා තවම සම්පූර්ණයෙන් සුවවුනේ නෑ, නුමුත් දැන් ටිකක් සනීපයි.

(b) I do not require any money now, but, if you can, send me some rice. Do not frighten the cows, which are eating grass in the garden. Tell the dhoby to bring my shirt to-morrow before 10 o'clock. Why did you refuse the vegetables sent to you yesterday by my friend. My bull was lost about 10 days after I went to my plumbago pit. When the thief entered my room a lamp was burning. The gentleman met me when I was walking on the road, near the boutique. Tell your children not to throw stones at my mango tree. The flight took place about an hour after sun set.

LESSON XXX. 30 පාඩම.

41. කියා, බව, that

129. Subordinate noun clauses are introduced in Sinhalese by the word **කියා**, when the verb in the subordinate clause is a finite one or a relative participle, or by බව, when the verb takes a gerundial form.

EXAMPLES. උදාහරණ.

වඩුවා පුටුව සාදනවාය කියා ඔහු මට කීවා, He told me that the carpenter is making the chair.

ඒ මිනිහා මැරුණාය කියා කව්දෝ මට කීවා, Some one told me that the man died.

ඔහු සිටින්නේ කොහේද කියා උඹ දන්නවාද ? Do you know where he is.

වඩුවා පුටුව සාදන බව ඔහු මට කීවා. He told me that the carpenter is making the chair.

ඒ මිනිහා මැරුණු බව මට ආරංචි උනා. I heard that the man died.

EXERCISE XXX. 30 අභ්‍යාසය පාඩම.

Transtate the following !—

(a) මේ මිනිහා මගේ වත්තේ වැට කැඩූවාය කියා මට ආරංචිඋනා. කොල්ලා කුඹුරට හරක් ඇතුල්කළ බව උඹට කීවේ කව්ද ? මේ මිනිස්සු දෙන්නා (දෙදෙනා) මගේ කුඹුරට හරකුන් ඇතුල්කළාය කියා මූලාදෑනියා මා සමග කීවා. ඌ පැමිනිලිකාරයාට පිහියෙන් ඇන්න බව මම දන්නවා. පැමිනිලිකාරයා විත්තිකාරයාව තල්ලුකළාය කියා එතන සිටි මිනිස්සු මා සමග කීවා. උඹේ මලයා නිතරම අරක්කු බීලා පාරේ පෙරළි කරනවාය කියා ගමේ මිනිස්සු කියනවා. පාන දුර පළාතේ තැනින් තැන කොලරා රෝගය පවතින බව ඒ පළාතේ විදාන ආරච්චිරාළ ඒජන්ත උන්නාන්සේට රපෝර්

තු කරලා තිබෙනවා. මේ ගමේ මිනීවලලන්ට සොහොන් බිමක් නැතිබව තමුසේ විසින් ආණ්ඩුවට දන්වන්ට ඕනෑ නොවේද? මගේ පලාතේ දූනට වසූරිය සහ සරම්ප බොහෝ කොට පවතින බවද මේ රෝගවලින් කීපදෙනෙක් පසුගිය සතියේ මළ බවද මම මුදියන්සේ රාළහාමිට රපෝර්තුකළා. මේ ගමේ සූදුකෙළිය හොර අරක්කු විකිණීම යන මේ ආදී දුසිරිත් පවතින බව මූලාදෑනි හොඳටම දන්නවා, නමුත් තක් කඩින්ට භයෙන් ඇහත් කනත් පියාගන ඉන්නවා. මගේ මස්සිනා ඇඟබද්ද ගෙවෙ නැත කියා විදෑන ආරච්චිරාළ අල්ලාගන ගිය බව මට දූන් ආරංචි උනා.

(a) All the people in the village say that your brother is a drunkard. Did you hear that your uncle died last night at Negombo? I think that the Headman of this village does not try to put down crime. The Headman has reported to me that there are several good plumbago lands in this village. Some one told me that there was a light burning in your house at 2 ǫ'clock last night. I heard some days ago that some thieves entered your house, but they could not take any valuable things. It is true that there are 15 arrack distilleries in the village of Potupitiya. Did you report to the Government Agent that epidemics are prevalent in the village a present,

---

LESSON XXXI. 31 පාඩම.

42. ගහනවා.

130. The verb ගහනවා takes various meanings according to the words with which it is joined.

EXAMPLES. උදාහරණ.

මේ ළමයා මට ගහනවා, this boy beats me.
මහත්මයා මට දඩගැහුවා, the gentleman fined me
මම පොතක් අච්චුගහනවා, I am printing a book.
ඌ මගේ මූණට කෙළ ගැහුවා, he spat on my face.

සීනුව ගහන්නේ කව්ද? who is ringing the bell?
කෑගහන්නේ කව්ද? who is crying out?
උඹේ අශ්වයා කොරගහනවා, your horse is limping.
හාවා හමගහන්ට කියා වැඩකාරයාට කියාපන්, tell the servant to skin the hare.

මම ඒ මිනිහාට අඬගැහුවා, I called that man.
මේ මස් ගඳගහනවා, this flesh stinks.
මිනිසුන්ට ගල්ගහන්ට එපා, do not throw stones at people.

EXERCISE XXXI. 31 අභ්‍යාස පාඩම.

Translate the following:—

(a). කැලෑවේ සතෙක් කෑගහනවා ඇසී මම ඒ දිහාවට හෙමින් හෙමින් ගියා. එතන ගඳක් ගැහූ නිසා මම ළමයින් අඬගහගන පාරට ආවා. නාකි මිනිහාගේ ගෙට ගල්ගැසූ මිනිසුන්ට නඩුකාර මහත්මයා එකාට රුපියල බැගින් දඩගැසුවා. මේ කොල්ලා පාරේ යන මිනිහෙකුගේ මූණට කෙළ ගැහුවාය කියා කඩකාරයා මා සමග කීවා. මගේ මස්සිනා රුපියල් පනහට ගත් ගොනා කොරගහනවාය කියා රුපියල් තිහකට වික්කා. දෙවෙනිවර සීනුව ගහන්ට පටන්ගත්තාම උඹලා පල්ලියට පලයල්ලා. පුරාණ කාලේ සමහර රජවරු මිනිසුන් හමගහලා මැරෙව්වාය කියා පොත්වල කියා තිබෙනවා. අච්චුගහපු පොත් මේ රටේ දැනට බොහොම භාවිතා වෙනවා. මේ මිනිහා පනාවක් ගහන්නේ උසාවියට හෝ කච්චේරියට යනකොට පමණයි.

LESSON XXXII. 32 පාඩම.

131. ගන්නවා, to take.

ගන්නවා with the past participle of a verb shews that the action is to the advantage of the Agent, as in **මම ජයගත්තා**, I had the victory; **උඹගෙයක් සදාගනින්**, make a house for yourself. **ගහගන්නවා** means strike each other, or fight and **බැනගන්නවා**, abuse each other.

EXERCISE XXXII. 32. අභ්‍යාස පාඩම.

Translate the following:—

(a.) මම අද උදේ ආණ්ඩුවේ මූකලාණෙන් ඉනි ටිකක් කපා ගෙන මගේ කුඹුරේ වැට බැඳගත්තා. මේ ගෙවල්වල මිනිස්සු නිතරම බැනගන්නවා. මේ මිනිස්සු දෙන්නා පාරේ ගහ ගත්තාය කියා මුලාදෑනියා උසාවියේදී කීවා. උඹලා අරක්කු බීලා පාරේ දබර කරගන්නේ මන්ද? මගේ පිහියේ ඊයේ රාත්‍රියේ තමුන්නාන්සේගේ වැඩකාරයා සොරකම්කරගෙන ගියාය කියා මට දැනගන්ට ලැබුණා. මම පැදුරක් සොයාගෙන මඩුවට ගොහින් පැය හතරක් පමණ නිදාගත්තා. මගේ පුතා සැම්දම ස්කෝලේට යන නුමුත් හොඳට ඉගනගන්නේ නැත කියා ගුරුන්නාන්සේ කියනවා. ළමයින්ට පැදුරු එලා ගෙන නිදාගන්ට කියාපන්. උඹ අප එනතුරු මේ ළමයින් බලාගන්ට ඕනෑ. මම බුරුත ලීවලින් හොඳ පුටුවක් සාදා ගත්තා.

(b) Tell the servant to keep my watch with him. Hov many hours a day do you sleep? I made a box (for myself) but I have no place to keep it. He built a house (for himself) in the Cinnamon Gardens, near the cemetery. The boys, who go to school regularly, will learn well. Tell these people not to fight on the public road, My cooly and the maid-servant frequently abuse (each other). When they were fighting in the compound I was only looking on. The thief took a bag of rice and rushed into the boutique. The two men were fighting on the road when the Policeman seized them. The drunkards remain on the road and quarrel, as the the tavern is kept open until 7 p.m.

APPENDIX.

1. Legal Terms.

Action, නඩුව.
Accused, දොෂාරොපනය කරන ලද අය.
Appeal, ඇපෑල.
Assignee, බලය ලත් අය.
Burglary, ගෙවල් උමංකෑම.
Bill of sale, විකුණුම් පත්‍රය.
Complain, පැමිණිලි කරනවා.
Complaint, පැමිණිල්ල.
Conveyance, සින්නාස්කරය.
Creditor, ණය හිමියා.
Court, උසාවිය.
Crminal Procedure Code, ක්‍රිමිනෙල්නඩු විධාන සංග්‍රහය
Civil Procedure Code, සිවෙල් නඩු විධාන සංග්‍රහය.
Damages, අලාභය.
Debtor, ණයකාරයා.
Decree, විනිශ්චය.
Deed of gift, තෑගි ඔප්පුව.
Deed of transfer, සින්නාස්කරය.
Defamation, කෙලහීම අපහාසය.
Defendant, විත්තිකාරයා.
Defence, විත්තිය.
Dismiss, නිෂ්ප්‍රභා කරනවා.
Divorce, දික්කසාදවීම, විවාහය අවලංගුවීම.
Ejectment, පිටකිරීම, අහක්කිරීම.
Evidence, සාක්ෂිය.
Fine, දඩය, දඩගහනවා.
Fiscal's Sale, පිස්කල් වෙන්දේසිය.
Highway robbery, මංකොල්ලය.
Immovable property, නිශ්චල දේපල.
Indictment, දෝෂාරෝපනය.
Injunction, තහනම.
Insolvency, වස්තුභංගත්වය.
Jurisdiction, අධිකාරය.

Issue (in a case) නිශ්චයකළයුතු දේ.
Lease, බද්ද.
Liability, බැඳිසිටීම, ණය.
Lessee, බදුගන්නා.
Last will, අසන්න පත්‍රය.
Lessor, බදු දෙන්නා.
Libel, කෙලසීම, පැමිණිලිපත්‍රය, අපහාසය.
Mortgage, උකස.
Mortgagee, උකස්හිමියා.
Moveable property, චඤ්චල දේපල.
Non-suit, නිෂ්ප්‍රභා කරනවා.
Ordinance, ආඥපනත.
Penal Code, දණ්ඩනීති සංග්‍රහය.
Plea, ගෙනහැර දක්වන කාරණය.
Prescription, භුක්තියේ අයිතිවාසිකම
Procedure, විභාග ක්‍රමය.
Procedings, විභාගයේ සටහන, නඩුපොත.
Rape, තනිස්නඩුව.
Rigorous imprisonment, බරපතල වැඩඇතුව හිරේදැමීම.
Section, කාණ්ඩය, වගන්තිය.
Summons, සිතාසිය.
Schedule, උපලේඛනය.
Seizure, ලියා තහනම්කිරීම.
Vagrant, පාදඩ.
Warrant, වරෙන්තුව.
Writ, ඇඤ්කීසිය.

---

2. Extract from a judgment.

This is an action by the plainliff to recover the value of a horse let to hire by him to the defendant, and which, it is alleged, died by reason of its having been immoderately used and over-driven. The horse was hired to the defendant to go a jurney of 24 miles and return, and the plaintiff alleges that the agreement was that the horse should have a day's rest before the return journey. The special agreement between the plaintiff and defendant that the horse should have a day's rest is not made the ground of the defendant's liability in this case. The plaintiff relied upon the implied condition in every contract of hiring that the hirer should use the thing hired with ordinary care.

Words.

Recover, අයකරගන්නවා Rest. පහසුව, නැවතිල්ල
Let to hire, කුලියටදුන්නා Ground, කාරණය
It is alleged, කියාසිටිනවා Relied, අදහගන සිටියා
[ලබන්නාවූ
By reason of, නිසා Implied, අදහස්කරනු
Immoderately, නිසිපමණින්වැඩිය Condition, නියමය [සුම
Overdriven, අධිකලෙසදක්කායාම Contract, ගනුදෙනුව, ගිවි
Agreement, පොරොන්දුව Ordinary, සාමාන්‍ය

Translation.

මේ (වනාහි) පැමිණිලිකාරයා විසින් විත්තිකාරයාට කුලියට දුන්නාවූද නිසි පමණට වැඩියෙන් පාවිච්චිකිරීම සහ අධිකලෙස දක්කායාම නිසා මැරුණාය කියා සිටින්නාවූද අශ්වයකුගේ වටිනාකම අයකරගන්ට පැමිණිලිකාරයා විසින් පමුණුවනලද නඩුවකි. හැතැප්ම 24 ක ගමනක් ගොස් එන පිණිස මේ අශ්වයා විත්තිකාරයාට කුලියට දෙන ලද්දේය. පොරොන්දුව නම් ආපසු එන්ට ප්‍රථමයෙන් අශ්වයාට දවසක් පහසුදෙන්ටයයි පැමිණිලිකාරයා කියා සිටිනවාය. පැමිණිලිකාරයා සහ විත්තිකාරයා අතරේවූ විශෙෂ පොරොන්දුව වන අශ්වයාට දවසක් පහසු දිය යුතුබව මේ නඩුවේ විත්ති කාරයා වග කියන්ට බැඳී සිටින කාරණයකොට ගෙන හැර දක්වානැත. කුලියට ගැනීමේ සියලු ගනුදෙනුවලදීම (යමක්) කුලියට ගන්නා අය තමා විසින් කුලියට ගන්නාලද දෙය සාමාන්‍ය ප්‍රවේසම ඇතුව පාවිච්චකාළ යුතු බව අදහස් කරනු ලබන්නාවූ නියමය පැමිණිලිකාරයා අදහාගන සිටියේය.

2 An Official Letter.

Sir,

I am directed by the Superintendent af Police, Western Province, to inform you that he has received an anonymous letter charging one Manis of Kanatta with the murder of a young man at the bridge of Nugegoda. The writer further states that the young man was strangled, robbed, and thrown into the Canal. You are requested to go to the spot at once and make careful inquiry as to the real facts of the case with a view to trace the offender and bring him to justie. If the body of the deceased has not already been found, you are to make careful search for it with the assistance of your petty headmen, and, if you succeed in discovering the body, you are to lose no time in reporting the matter to the Coroner of the District. The result of your inquiries is to be communicated to the superintendent of the place with as little delay as possible.

I am Sir,

Your Obedient Servant,

MARADANA,
22nd April, 1202.

Translation.

මහත්මයාණෙනි,

නුගේගොඩ පාලම ළඟදී තරුණ මිනිහෙකු මැරුවාය කියා කානත්තේ මානිස් යන අයෙකුට විරුඩව දෝෂාරෝපනයක් දක්වා තිබෙන නිර්නාමක ලියමනක් ලැබී තිබෙන බව තමුසේට දක්වන්ට කියා බස්නාහිර පළාතේ පොලිස් සුපිරින්ටැන්ඩන්ට්තුමා විසින් මට නියම කරන්ට යෙදුනා ඇත. ඒ තරුණ මිනිහාව මරා බඩු සොරකම් කරගෙන ඇළට විසිකරදමා තිබෙන බව ලියුම්කරුවා වැඩි දුරටත් කියන්නේය. තමුසේ වහාම ඒ ස්ථානයටගොස් අපරාධකාරයා සොයා නඩු මාග්ගයට පමුණුවන පිණිස මේ කාරණයේ හරි සිඩිය කෙසේද කියා ප්‍රවේසමෙන් විභාගකරන ලෙස ඕනෑ කෙරේ. මැරුණු අයගේ ශරීරය මේතාක් සම්බවී නැත්නම් තමුසේගේ සුළු මුලාදෑනීන්ගේ උපකාර ඇතුව හොඳකාර සෝදිසි කළ

යුතුයි. ශරීරය සොයාගැන්ම හැකිවිනම් දිස්ත්‍රික්කේ කෝර්නර් තැනට රපෝර්ති කිරීම ගැන කල්ගත නොකල යුතුයි. තමුසේගේ විභාගයෙන් දැනගන්ට ලැබෙන කාරණා හැකිතරම් අප්‍රමාදව පොලිස් සුපිරින්ටැන්ඩන්ට් තුමාට දැනුම්දිය යුතුයි.

APPENDIX II.

Sinhalese Idiomatic Phrases.

මට බෑ, I cannot
මට පොතක් තිබෙනවා, I have a book
මා ළඟ මුදල් නෑ, I have no money
මා ළඟ සිටි වැඩකාරයා, the servant who was with me
මේ මිනිහාගේ ඇහැ පෙනෙන්නේ නෑ, this man is blind
උඹේ කන ඇහෙන්නේ නැද්ද? are you deaf?
මගේ පුතා බීමට වැටිලා ඉන්නවා, my son has taken to drink
ඒ මිනිහා එල්ලෙන්ට හැදුවා, that man attempted to hang himself
මගේ පුතාලෙඩින් වැටීලා සුමාන තුනක් වෙනවා, it is three weeks since my son fell ill
උඹට මතක නැද්ද? do yon not remember
අද එන්ට හදපන්, try to come to-day
මට ඇහුම්කන්දියන්, listen to me
මට ඇහැන්නේ නෑ, I do not hear
ඒක අත්වැරැද්දෙන් උනා, it was done unintentionally
මේ වැඩේට මාසයක් අල්ලයි, it will take a month to do this work
මේ මිනිහා ගස් යනවා, this man climbs trees
ලෙඩාට සනීපවේගෙන එනවා, the sick man is recovering
මට කමක් නෑ, I do not care
ළඟදී මම ගමට ගියා, I went to the village lately
රෑට නිදි මරන්ට එපා, do not keep up at night
ඒකට මට මොකද? what is that to me?
නිකම් ඉඳින්, keep quiet
ඒ මිනිහා හොරෙක් නොවේයැයි, is not that man a thief? (surely that man is a thief)

ඔහු මට ගහන්ට සැදුවා, he threatened to beat me

ඊයේ බොහොම වැහි වැස්සා, there was much rain yesterday

මම ගොහින් එන්නං I shall go and come

ඔයාකාර පල්බොරු කියන්ට එපා, do not tell such rank lies

ඔහු කිසි දෙයක් මා දක්කදී කිවේ නෑ, he did not tell me any thing

මට උඹ ආවත් එකයි නාවත් එකයි, it is all the same to me whether you come or not

මම ඉඳලා හිටලා ගමට යනවා I go to the village occasionally

වසංගතය ඉක්මනින් බෝවේගන යනවා, the epidemic is fast spreading

මිනිස්සු දහයක් වාගේ හිටියා, there were about 10 men

මේක ඉබේම කැඩෙන්ට බෑ, this cannot break itself

ඔහු මට කුණුහරුපෙන් බැන්නා, he abused me in indecent language

ඔහු බලි පාරට වැටුනා, he fell on his back

ඔහු ටිකකදී ගඟේ වැටෙනවා, he was very nearly falling into the river

මට ගස් යන්ට බෑ, I cannot climb trees

ඔහු අව්ව තපිනවා, he is basking in the sun

ඔහු ඇනතියා ගන ඉන්නවා, he squats

ඔහු දත්මිටි කනවා, he is gnashing the teeth

උඹට මක්වෙලාද? what is the matter with you?

මම එනකල්හිටපන්, wait till I come

උඹ කමකට නැති ලමයෙක්, you are a good for nothing boy

ඒ මිනිහා ගැහුම් කෑවා, that man had a beating

මම වැටෙන්ට ගියා, I was nearly falling

ඔහු යම්තම් බේරුනා, he had a narrow escape

මට මතකනෑ, I do not remember

මේ පොත කාගේද? whose book is this?

උඹ කව්ද? who are you?

මේක ඕනෑ කාටද, who wants this

මේ පොත උඹට කොයින්ද? where did you get this book from?

ඕක මොකවද? what is this for?

උඹට දැන් සනීපද? are you well now?

තෝ හොරෙකි, you are a thief

කල්තියා වරෙන්, come in time

උඹට ළමයි කීදෙනෙක් ඉන්නවාද? how many children have you?

උඹට කුඹුරු කීයක් තිබෙනවාද ? how many fields have you?

ඔහු වැඩකරනවා මම දුටුවා, I saw him work

ලියා ඔප්පුකරන රපෝර්තුවයි, report written and submitted

මම මේ මිනිහා අඳුනන්නේ නෑ, I do not know this man

මම හොරාව ඇඳින්නේ නෑ, I did not recognize the thief

උඹ ගනතේ කීදෙනෙක් වැඩකරනවාද? how many men work under you?

අළුත්පිට මේක විකුණන්ට පුළුවනි, this can be sold while new

ඔහු වැඩකරන්නේ අවට ගියාවයි, he works in a slip-shod way

ඔහු ගෙදර යන ගමන් මෙහාට ගොඩවැදුනා, on his way home he stepped in here

අර හොරා ගේමයි, that is the thief I suppose

ඒක මා අතින් කැඩුනා, it was broken my me unintentionally

උඹ ලෙලිපොල් මිලේට ගන්නවාද? do you buy unhusked cocoanuts?

ඔහු ආ ගමන්ම මට ගැහුවා, he struck me as soon as he came

ඔහු එහෙමත් දවසක පල්ලියට යනවා, he goes to church only occasionally

ඔහු එසේ මෙසේ කෙනෙක් නොවෙයි, he is not an ordinary person

මට අවසර, I take your leave

මේ ගමේ මම දන්නේ එහෙමත් කෙනෙකි, I know only a very few persons in this village

ඔහු ඇහැත් කනත් පියාගන ඉන්නවා, he is conniving at (it)

කෝ බලන්ට, let me see

ඔහු දවස තිස්සේම නිදියෙනවා, he sleeps the whole day

ඒකට මගේ අත පොවන්නේ නෑ, my hand does not reach it

ඒක උගේ ඇබ්බෑසිය, it is his habit

මේක අත්දැකපු බේතකි, this is a tried medicine

ඔහු අත්හදා බලන්ට යනවා, he is going to experiment

මගේ ගොනා වත්තේදිග එළි කර තිබූනා, my bull was tethered in the garden.

ඒක එහෙම පිටින්ම වැරදියි, this is entirely wrong

ගිය අවුරුද්දේ මම මේ හේන වැඩකළා, I cultivated this chena, last year

එන මාසේ මම ගමට යනවා, I go to the village next month

උඹ මට තානායමේ ඉඳුම් හිටුම් ලෑස්තිකළාද? have you prepared lodgings for me in the rest House?

ඔහු උඩුබැල්ලෙන් වැටුණා, he fell on his back (he fell looking up)

ඌ හෙළුවැල්ලෙන් හිටියා, he was naked

මට නිදිමතයි, I feel sleepy

ඔහු රෑබෝවෙලා ගෙදර ආවා, he came home late in the night

මගේ පුතා වල්වෙලා ඉන්නවා, my son has taken to bad ways

මේ මිනිස්සු රෑ පානේ ඇවිදිනවා,, these men walk in the moon-light night

කැලෑව ගනසැරේ වැවිලා තිබුණා, jungle was grown thickly

Vocabulary, Sinhalese and English.

(අ.)

අක්කරය, acre
අක්කා, elder sister
අකුසල්, sin .
අගම්, augmentation
අගල, ditch
අඟ, horn
අඟහරුවාදා, Tuesday
අගෝස්තු, August
අච්චුකරනවා, to punish
අට, eight
අටවක, the 8th day after the new or full moon
අඩිය, foot
අඬනවා, cry
අණ, command
අත්ත, branch
අත්පා, hand and foot
අත්පොත, hand book
අත, hand
අතන, there
අතරතුර, during
අතිරික්ත, exceeding
අතුරනවා, to spread
අද, to-day
අදිනවා, to drag
අදියර, chapter
අධිගත, gone over
අධිපතියා, chief
අඳිනවා, to dress
අන්අරුත්සමස්, relative compounds
අනාදර, injustice
අනිච්චවත්, alas
අනිද්දා, day after to-morrow
අනිනවා, to butt
අනුචර, attendant
අනුබල, support
අනුමත, consent
අන්‍යපසමාස, relative compounds
අප්‍රියෙල්, April
අප්පා, father
අපදත්, taking away
අපි, we
අපේ, our
අපොයි, alas
අබිදම්, metaphysics
අභිමුඛ, presence
අඹරනවා, to twist
අම්මා, mother
අමාවක, new moon
අමුණ, five bushels
අයියා, elder brother
අයෙක්, person
අර, that
අරක්කු, arrack
අරිනවා, to open, to send
අල්ලනවා, to catch
අල්ලස්, bribe
අලියා, elephant
අලුත්, new
අව්‍යයසමාස, indeclinable compounds
අවනම්බු, dishonour
අවවාද, advice
අවසන්, conclusion
අව්‍යයසමස්, indeclinable compounds
අවුරුදු, years
අශ්වයා, horse
අස්වැන්න, crops

අසරණ, helpless
අසූව, eighty
අහක, away
අහසෙහි, in the sky
අහුවෙනවා, to be caught
අළු, ashes

(ආ)

ආකාශය sky
ආගම, augmentation
ආගමන, coming
ආච්චි, grand mother
ආඥපනත, ordinance
ආඥව, order
ආවා, came
ආවාවේ, let him come
ආප්ප, hoppers
ආශ්වාස, inhaled air

(ඇ)

ඇඟ, body
ඇත්ත, truth
ඇත්තවම, truly
ඇතා elephant
ඇතින්න, ඇතිනි } she elephant
ඇතිකරනවා, to rear, bring up
ඇතුල්වෙනවා, to enter
ඇතුල්කරනවා, to put in
ඇද්ද, dragged
ඇදිල්ල, ඇදීම, ඇදුම, } the dragging
ඇඳ, bed
ඇන්නා, stabbed
ඇපෑල, appeal
ඇයි, why
ඇරත්, besides
ඇරියා, sent
ඇවිත්, ඇවිදින් } having come
ඇවිදිනවා, walk
ඇසල, July
ඇස, eye
ඇහෙනවා, hear
ඇළ, canal

(ඈ)

ඈ, she
ඈත, afar
ඈලා, they

(ඉ)

ඉක්මනින්, quickly
ඉඩම, land
ඉත්ත, twig
ඉතාම, very

ඉතින්, and then, after that
ඉදිමෙනවා, to swell
ඉදිරිපිට, before
ඉත්අනිද්දා, three days hence
ඉන්න, fence stick
ඉන්නිසා, therefore
ඉපදෙනවා to be born
ඉබ්බා, tortoise
ඉබේට } by chance
ඉබේම }
ඉර, line, sun
ඉරනවා, to tear, to saw
ඉරිදා, Sunday
ඉල්, November
ඉලන්දාරියා, young man
ඉලව්වෙව්, death! (expressing horror)
ඉවත, aside
ඉෂ්ටකරනවා, to accomplish
ඉස්සර, of old, before
ඉස්සරහ, in front
ඉහල, above

(ඊ.)

ඊරි, sow
ඊයේ, yesterday

(උ.)

උග්ගස්, sugar cane
උගනී, he learns
උඩ, on, above
උඩල, a kind of yam
උණුකරනවා, to boil
උණුවතුර, hot water
උත්සාහකලා, tried
උද්ග්‍රහණ, learning
උදාහරණ, examples
උදුරනවා, to snatch
උදේ, morning
උඳුවක් } December
උඳුවප් }
උන්නාන්සේ } he
උන්නැහේ }
උන්නාන්සේලා } they
උන්නැහෙලා }
උපඒජන්ත, Assistant Agent
උපක්‍රමය, means
උපදිනවා, to be born
උපලේඛනය, schedule
උපවන, neighbouring forest
උපසර්ග, prefixes
උඹ } you
උඹලා }
උමග, tunnel
උයනවා, to cook
උලව්වෙව්, death. (expressing horror
උස්, high, tall

(ඌ.)

ඌ, he,
ඌරා, pig,
ඌලා, they

(එ.)

එතකල්, until then
එතකොට, then
එතන, there
එදා, that day
එනවා, to come
එපමණ, that much
එපාකරනවා, to reject, refuse
එබැවින්, therefore
එළගෙරක්, cattle, in contradistinction to buffaloes
එහෙත්, but
එහෙම, in that manner
එළුවා, goat

(ඒ.)

ඒකී, she
ඒනිසා, therefore
ඒයි, used in addressing another

(ඔ.)

ඔක්තෝබර්, October
ඔතනවා, wrap round
ඔපමණ, so much
ඔබ, yonder
ඔබමොබ, here and there
ඔය, that
ඔරුව, boat
ඔව්හු, they
ඔහු, he

(ඕ.)

ඕනෑකරනවා, to require
ඕයි, used in addressing another

(ක.)

කියනවා, it pains
කට, mouth
කටිනවා, spin
කටුවල, a kind of yam
කඩකරනවා, to violate,
කඩකාරයා, boutique keeper
කඩදාසිය, paper
කඩනවා, to break
කඩිනමට, soon
කඩුව, sword
කඩේ, boutique
කාණා, blind man

කථාකරනවා, to speak
කඳ, trunk of a tree, body
කන්තෝරුව, office
කන්ද, mountain
කන, ear
කනවා, to eat
කපනවා, to cut
කපුටා crow
කඹේ, rope
කරත්තේ, cart
කරනවා, to do
කරමින්, doing
කර්තෘ විභක්තිය, instrumental case
කර්ම විභක්තිය, accusative case
කලඳ, drachm
කලාතුරකින්, seldom
කලින්කල, from time to time
කව්ද, who
කවදාද, when
කසාදබඳිනවා, to marry
කහිනවා, to cough
කළ, done
කළු, black
කාගේද, whose
කාගෙන්ද, from whom
කාටද, to whom
කාසි, money
කැටුව, with
කැරපියා, cockroach
කැලේ, jungle
කෑම, food
කෑවා, ate
කිමිදිනවා, to dive
කියනවා, to say
කියවනවා, to read
කිරි, milk
කිවිනි, O poets
කිලුටු, dirty
කීකරු. obedient
කීම, saying
කුකුළා, cock
කුඩම්මා, aunt
කුඩා, small
කුඩේ, umbrella
කුඹුරු, fields
කුරුණිය, $\frac{1}{8}$ of a bushel
කුරුඳු, cinnamon
කුරුල්ලා, bird
කෙන්ද, fibre
කෙර, lame woman
කෙල්ල, lass
කෙළිනවා, to play
කොකා, crane
කොට, short
කොටනවා, to cnt, to dig
කොටස, share
කොටා, shortman
කොටියා, cheetah
කොඳුරනවා, to whisper
කොයි, which
කොයිබද, where
කොරා, lame man
කොල්ලා, lad
කොහෙත්ම, at all
කොහේද, where
කොහොම, how
කොහොමවත්, any how
කොළ, leaves
කොළොම්පුර, Colombo
කෝකද, which

(ග)

ගඟ, river
ගතකුරු, consonants
ගන්නවා, to take
ගම, villaga
ගල, stone
ගලකින්, with a stone
ගලනවා, to flow
ගවයන්, cattle
ගහ, tree
ගහනවා, to beat
ගානවා, to rub
ගැබ, womb
ගෑනියක්, a woman
ගිරවා, parrot
ගිලිනවා, to swallow
ගෙත්තම්, weaving
ගෙදර, home
ගෙය, house
ගොක්කොළ, tender cocoanut [leaves
ගොනා, ox, bull
ගොවිතැන, cultivation
ගොවියා, cultivator
ගොයම, corn
ගොළුවා, dumb man
ගංඉවුර, river bank
ගංවතුර, river water

(ණ.)

ණය, debt

(ත.)

තණ, grass
තණබිම් grass land
තදින් } strongly
තදේට }
තනියම, alone
තඹ, copper
තමුසේ, you
තමුන්නාන්සේ, you, respect- [ful
තරුණ, young
තරුණයා, young man
තල්ලුකරනවා, to shove
තව } more
තවත් }
තවද, moreover
තවම, still
තැනින්තැන, from place to [place
තැබෑරුම, tavern
තෑග්ග, present
තිරිසනා, brute
තී, you
තීලා, you
තුඩ, beak
තුන්වෙනුව, thirdly
තුන්ලෝ, the three worlds
තුනක්, three
තුරු, untill
තෙල්, oil
තොප්පිය, hat
තොපි, you

(ද.)

තෝ, you
ද, and
දඅරුත්සමස්, } collective
දකාරඑසමාස } compounds
දඩාවතේ, astray
දඬුවම්, punishment
දණ, knee
දනවා, to burn
දරු, child
දරුවන්, children
දරුවෙනි, O children
දවස්පතා, daily
දවස, day
දා, day
දාසයා, slave
දැක්කා, saw
දැන්, now
දැනට, for the present
දැනෙනවා to feel
දික්, long
දින, day
දිනිඳු, sun
දිමියා, red ant
දියවෙනවා, to be dissolved
දිලිසෙනවා, to swear
දිවියා, leopard
දිවුරනවා, to swear
දී, at, when
දුක, grief
දුකින්, with grief
දුදන, bad men, wicked men
දුක්, grief
දුප්පත්, poor
දුබල, powerless
දුඹුරු. brown
දුගීන්ධ, bad smell
දුරුතු, January
දුවණියෝ, daughter
දුවනවා, to run
දුශ්චරිත, vice
දූ, daughter
දෙන, cow
දෙනවා. to give
දෙවනු, rfterwards
දෙවියෝ, God
දෙළ, brook

(න)

නගරවාසී, citizen
නගා, younger sister
නගිනවා, to asecnd
නගුල, plough
නපුරු, wicked
නපුංසක, neuter
නටනවා, to dance
නයා, cobra
නරක්කරනවා, to spoil
නරක, bad
නරනිඳු, monarch
නරියා, fox

නවතිනවා, to remain
නවම්, February
නාකි, old
නානවා, to bathe
නාමප්‍රකෘති, stems of nouns
නැගිටිනවා, to rice up
නැත්නම්, if not
නැන්දෑ, mother in-law, paternal aunt
නැතිකරනවා, to ruin, to lose
නැව, ship
නැවත, again
නැවතිල්ලේ, slowly
නැළිය, $\frac{1}{32}$ part of a bushel
නැංගා, ascended
නැ, no
නැනා, sieter in-law
නිකම් without work
නිකිණි, August
නිතර, always
නිදියෙනවා, to sleep
නිදහස්කරනවා, to release
නිදොස්, without fault
නිපාත, indeclinable words
නියර, ridge dam
නිදෝෂ, without fault
නිරන්තර, always
නිරවුල්, undisturbed
නිල්, blue
නිලුපුල්, blue lotus
නිවැරදි, guiltless
නිෂ්ඵල, fruitless, useless
නීච, mean
නුමුත්, but
නුවණැති, having wisdom
නූල, thread
නොකඩව, continuoasly, regularly
නොහොත්, or

(ප.)

ප්‍රත්‍යුත්තර, reply
ප්‍රමාණය, extent
ප්‍රයෝජ්‍යක්‍රියා, the causal verb
ප්‍රාශ්වාස, expirated breath
ප්‍රාණවාච, animate
පඩි, wages
පඩිතුමා, erudite person
පණ, life
පණකුරු, vowels
පණුවා, worm
පදිනවා, to row
පනිනවා, to jump
පරණ, old
පරපුටු, beggar, cuckoo
පරාවා, a kind of fiish
පරාජය, defeat
පරිපූර්ණ, perfect
පල්ලිය, church
පව්කාරයා, sinner, sinful man
පව, sin
පවතිනවා to last
පවර, great
පස්, earth
පස්සේ, afterwards
පසළොස්වක, full moon day

පසැස්, name of Buddha alluding to his five faculties of perception
පසුව, afterwards
පසිදු, famous
පලමුදා, the third day back
පාගනවා, to trample upon
පාඩම, lesson
පාර, road
පාලම, bridge
පාවෙනවා, to float
පැදුර, mat
පැනපිය, jump, imp.
පැණි, honey
පැමිණිල්ල, plaint
පැය, hour
පැරදුම, defeat
පැසෙනවා, to ripen
පැල, measure equal to ten kurunis
පිට, out
පිදුරු, straw
පිනැති, meritorious, lucky
පිපිරෙනවා, to burst
පිම්බා, blew
පිඹිනවා, to blow
පියදු කිරිය, the causal verb
පියා, father
පියාණෝ, father
පියාගන, having closed
පියාඹනවා, to fly
පිරිවර, retinue
පිස්සා, mad man
පිහිනවා, to sweep
පිහියෙන්, with the knife
පිළිතුරු, reply
පිළිපදිනවා, to observe
පිළියම්, remedy
පීනනවා, to swim
පුටුව, chair
පුතාණෝ, son
පුනරුක්ත, tautology
පුරුෂයා, man, husband
පුළුස්සනවා, to burn
පුවක්, arecanut
පෙට්ටිය, box
පෙනෙනවා, to appear
පෙබරවාරි, February
පෙරෙයිදා, the day before yesterday
පොත, book
පොද, drop
පොල්තෙල්, cocoanut oil
පොල්ල, club
පොල් වත්ත, cocoanut estate
පොසොම්, June
පෝය, quarters of the moon
පංගුව, share
පුංචි, small

(බ.)

බ්‍රහස්පතින්දා, Thursday
බක්, April
බඩ, belly
බඩු, goods
බත්, boiled rice
බතල, sweet potatoes

බදාදා, Wednesday
බදිනවා, to fry
බදුඔප්පුව, lease
බඳිනවා, to bind
බනිනවා, to abuse
බබලනවා, to shine
බමුණා brahmin
බල්ලා, dog
බලෙන් } by force
බලේට }
බස්නාහිර, west
බහිනවා, to descend
බහු, plural
බළලා, cat
බාගවෙලාවට, sometimes
බාන, pair
බාල, young
බැටළුවා, sheep
බැල්ලී, bitch
බෑ, cannot
බෑනා, sister's son, son in-law
බිණර, Septembr
බිත්තරවී, seed padddy
බිඳිනවා, to break
බිම්කට්ටිය, portion of land
බිසව, queen
බුරනවා, to bark
බූරුවා, ass
බෙල්ල, neck
බෙල්ලා, oyster
බේබද්දා, drunkard
බොන්නා, drunkard
බොනවා, to drink
බොරුකාරයා, liar
බොල } used in address
බොලන් } ing another
බොහොම, much
බොහෝකොට, greatly

(හ.)

හයවෙනවා, to be frightened

(ම.)

මකුණා, bug
මග, way
මගේ, my
මට, to me
මත්තට, in the future
මත්වෙනවා, to become intoxicated
මදක්, a little
මන්ද, why
මනා, good
මනාව, } weel
මනාසේ, }
මනිනවා, to measure
මම, I
මල, flower
මලයා, younger brother
මව්පියෝ, parents
මව, mother
මස්, flesh
මස්සිනා brother-in-law
මහ, one of the harvests
මහත්මයා, gentleman
මහනවා to sew
මහල්ලා oldman
මහා, great

මහොත්තම, great
මාමා, maternal uncle, father-in-law
මාර්තු, March
මාළු, fish
මාසය, month
මැඩියා, frog
මැණික, gem
මැතිඳු, minister of state
මැදින්දින } March
මැදින් } March
මැයි, May
මැරුනාවේ, let him die
මැරෙනවා, to die
මැස්සා, fly
මැහැල්ල, old woman
මැණියෝ, mother
මැතදී, lately
මිටි, short
මිනිරන්, plumbago
මිතුරා, friend
මින්මතු, hereafter
මිනිත්තුව, minute
මිනිස්සු, men
මිනිසා } man
මිනිහා } man
මීයා, rat
මීහරකා, buffalo
මුනුබුරා, grandson
මුල, root
මුවා, deer
මූ, this one
මූණ, face
මෘගයා, beast
මෙතන, here
මෙලහකට, by this time
මෙසේ, thus
මෙහි, here
මේ, this
මොකද, what
මොනරා, peacock
මොහොත, moment
මොහොර, rampart
මෝසම, harvest time

ය

යකඩ, iron
යකා, devil
යට, under
යතුර, key
යන්තම්, narrowly,
යනවා, go
යල, one of the harvests
යහපත්, good
යහපත්කොට, well
යහමින්, abundantly
යහළුවා, friend
යාකරනවා, to connect

(ර.)

රජ්ජුරුවෝ, king
රජතුමා, great king
රජාණෝ, king
රතු, red

රදවා, washer-man, dhoby
රන්, gold
රා, toddy
රැවටෙන්ට, to be deceived
රැල, wave
රෑට, to-night
රිදී, silver
රිලවා, monkey
රෙද්ද, cloth

(ල.)

ලබනවා, to receive
ලමයා, boy
ලමිස්සි, young woman
ලාහ, measure of quantity equal to 4 nelis
ලැබෙනවා, to obtain
ලිප්ගල්, hearth stones
ලිඞ්ග } gender
ලිඟු }
ළිඳ, well
ලිප, hearth
ලිය, woman
ලියනවා, write
ලියැද්ද, division of a paddy field
ලෙඩා, patient
ලෙම්බ, mare
ලේ, blood
ලේලි, niece, daughter-in-law
ලොකු, big
ලොවට, to the world
ලෝකාර්ථ, public good

(ව.)

වක්, October
වක්කරනවා, to pour
වගුරනවා, to shed
වටිනවා, is worth
වටේට, around
වඩිනවා, to go (respectful)
වඩුවා, carpenter
වත්, or
වත්ත, garden
වතුර, water
වදාරනවා, to say
වදිනවා. rush in, hit against
වඳිනවා, worship
වඳුරා, ape
වප්, October
වපසරිය, sowing extent
වපුරනවා, to sow
වමැස, left eye
වරදිනවා, to err
වරින්වර, from time to time
වළඳ, pan
වලසා } bear
වලහා }
වවුලා, bat
වස්සා, calf
වසිනවා, to rain
වහනවා, to cover
වහාම, forthwith

වහිනවා, to rain
වළ, pit
වළලනවා, to bury
වාගේ, like
වැට, fence
වැටෙනවා, to fall
වැඩකරනවා, to work
වැඩකාරයා, man-servant
වැඩකාරී, maid-servant
වැඩිපුර, over and above
වැඩිය, more
වැඩේ, work
වැද්දා, hunter
වැඳිරි, ape (female)
වැපුරුවා, sowed
වැරෙන් } strongly
වැරේට }
වැලහිනී, she-bear
වැලි sand
වැව, tank
වැවෙනවා, to grow
විකුණනවා, to sell
විචාරනවා, to enquire
විටින්විට, from time to time
විපත, calamity

විබත්, case
විබත්සමස් } case compounds
විභක්තිසමාස }
වියදම්කරනවා, to spend
වියනවා, to weave
වියවුල්, confusion
වියෝග disunion
විලාසය, form
විශෙෂණසමාස, adjectival compounds
විසින්, by
වී, paddy
වීගොවිතැන, paddy cultivation
වීසිකරනවා, to throw
වීසිවෙනවා, to be thrown
වෙඩිතබනවා, to fire at
වෙදා, medical man
වෙනම, separately
වෙනවා, to become
වෙල, field
වෙසක්, May
වෙසෙසුන් සමස්, adjectival compounds
වෙළඳ, merchant
වෙළඹ, mare
වේල්ල, dam
වේලාසනින්, early

(ශ.)

ශතපත්‍ර, lotus
ශබ්ද, voice

(ස.)

ස්කෝලය, school
ස්ත්‍රී, woman, wife
සණ්ඩුකරනවා, quarrel
සත්තකට, truly, surely
සත්තු, animals
සතිය, week

සතුරා, enemy
සඳුදා, Monday
සන්ධි, combination
සබඳ, connected
සම්පූර්ණ, perfcel
සම්බවෙනවා to meet
සම්බන්ධ, connected
සම්බකරනවා, to earn
සමග, with
සමහරවිට, sometimes
සමාස, compounds
සර්පයා, serpent
සරසනවා, to decorate
සසර, metempsychosis
සහ, and, with
සහෝදරයෝ, brothers
සාදනවා, to make
සැඟවෙනවා, conceal
සැනසෙනවා, to be consoled
සැප්තැම්බර්, September,
සැප, comfort
සැපෙන්, comfortably
සැබැවට, truly
සැමදම, everyday
සිකුරාදා, Friday
සිටපුවාවේ, let him stay
සිටිනවා, to stand
සිත්තරු, painters
සිඩවෙනවා, to take place
සිනාසෙනවා, to laugh
සිඹිනවා, to kiss
සිව්පාවෝ, quadrupeds
සිවුරඟ, four-fold
සිහිල්, cold
සීනි. sugar
සීයා, grandfather
සුගන්ධ, good smell
සුදන, good men
සුදු, white
සුදුසු, fit, proper
සුමානය, week
සුවඳ, good smell
සුවවෙනවා, to be cured
සූදුකෙළිනවා, to gamble
සූරනවා, to scrape
සෙනසුරාදා, Saturday
සෙල්ලම්කරනවා, to play
සේරුව, measure $\frac{1}{32}$ part of a bushel
සොරකම්කරනවා, to steal
සොරබිය, fear arising from thieves
සොරු, thieves
සෝදනවා, to wash
සංගම, association
සිංහයා, lion

(හ.)

හරක්, cattle
හරක්මස්, beef
හරකා, ox
හරකී, cow
හරි, or, right
හරහට, across
හා, and, with
හාත්පසින්, on all sides
හානවා, to plough
හාරනවා, to dig

හාල්, unboiled rice
හැඟෙනවා, to perecive
හැන්ද, spoon
හිඟුරල, a kind of yam
හිතොපදෙශ, proverbs
හිරසඳ, sun and moon
හිස්ඹිඩම්, waste land
හිස, head
හුළඟ, wind
හෙට, tomorrow
හෙමින්, slowly
හෙවත්, alias
හෙලිල්ලඹු, white women
හේන, chena–land
හොඳ, good
හොරා, thief
හොරෙන්, stealthily
හෝ,or

(ළං)

ළඟට, near
ළඟදී, lately
ළංවෙනවා, to approach

Vocabulary, English and Sinhalese.

A.

Abundantly, බොහෝකොට
Abuudance, රාශිය
About, පමණ
Above, ඉහළ
Abuse, *v.* බනිනවා
Accept, පිළිගන්නවා
Accomplish, ඉෂ්ටකරනවා
Acre, අක්කරය
Across, හරහා
Adjoin, යාවෙනවා
After, පසුව
Afterwards, දෙවනු, පසුව
Afar, ඈත
Again, නැවත
Alias, හෙවත්
Alas, අපොයි
Alonc, තනියම්
And, ද, ත්, තවද
August, අගෝස්තු
April, අප්‍රියෙල්
Apc, වඳුරා
Appendix, උපලේඛනය
Arecanut, පුවක්
Around, වටේට
Arrack, අරක්කු
Ashes, අළු
Ass, බූරුවා
Aside, ඉවත

Astray, දඩාවතේ
Ascend, නගිනවා
Association, සමාගම, සංගම
At, ද
At all, කොහෙත්ම
Aunt, නැන්දා, කුඩම්මා

B

Bad, නරක,
Bag, මල්ල
Bat, වවුලා
Bathe, නානවා
Bank, ඉවුර
Bark, බුරනවා
Bear, වලහා
Beast, මෘගයා
Beak, තුඩ
Beat, ගහනවා
Become, වෙනවා
Bed, ඇඳ
Before, ඉස්සර
Below, පහල
Belly, බඩ
Beggar, හිඟන්නා
Big, ලොකු
Bind, බඳිනවා
Bird, කුරුල්ලා
Blind, කණ
Blood, ලේ
Black, කළු
Blue, නිල්,
Boy, ලමයා
Boat, ඔරුව
Born, උපදිනවා
Boil { උණුකරනවා / තම්බනවා,
Boutique, කඩේ
Body, ශරීරය
Box, පෙට්ටිය
Book, පොත
Branch, අත්ත
Brahmin, බමුණා
Brute, තිරිසනා
Bridge, පාලම
Bribe, අල්ලස්
Brother, සහෝදරයා
Brother-in-law මස්සිනා
Break, කඩනවා
Brook, දොළ
Bring, ගෙනෙනවා
Bundle, මිටිය
Burn, පුළුස්සනවා
But, නුමුත්
Bull, ගොනා
Bug, මකුණා
Burst, පුපුරනවා
Bury, වළලනවා
Buffalo, මීහරකා
Bushel, බුසල
Buy, මිලේටගන්නවා
By, විසින්

C

Canal ඇළ
Cannot, බැහැ, බැ
Cat, බළලා
Calf, වස්සා

Catch, අල්ලනවා
Carpenter, වඩුවා
Cattle, ගවයෝ
Caused, සැලැස්සුවා
Cart, කරත්තේ [වූ
Called, අඩගැසුවා, කියන, නම්
Cemetery, සොහොන්බිම, මිනී පිට්ටනිය
Chena, හේන
Chance, ඉබේ
Chair, පුටුව
Cheetah, දිවියා, කොටියා
Citizen, නගරවාසී
Club, පොල්ල
Cock, කුකුලා
Cockroach, කැරපියා
Cobra, නයා

Cow, එලදෙන, හරකී
Come, එනවා,
Copper, තඹ
Cook, උයන්නා, කෑම් පිසන්නා
Cooly, කුලීකාරයා
Cough, කැස්ස
Console, සනසනවා
Conceal, සඟවනවා
Cocoanut, පොල්
Comb, පනාව
Compound, මිදුල
Corn, ගොයම
Crop, අස්වැන්න
Construct, සාදනවා
Comfort, පහසු
Crow, කපුටා

D

Dam, වේල්ල
Dance, නටනවා
Daily, දවස්පතා
Day, දවස
Daughter, දූ
Daughter-in-law ලේලි
Dead, මළ
December, දෙසැම්බර්
Deer, මුවා
Descend, බහිනවා
Devil, යකා
District, දිස්ත්‍රික්කේ, පලාත
Distillery, කල්දේරම්මඩුව
Die, මැරෙනවා

Dirty, කිලුටු
Dig, හාරනවා
Do, කරනවා
Dhoby. රදවා
Dog, බල්ලා
Do not, එපා
Do not want, එපා
Drag, අදිනවා
Drunkard, බේබද්දා
Drink, බොනවා
Drop, පොද
Dumb, ගොළු
Dumb man, ගොළුවා
During, අතරතුර

E

East, නැගෙනහිර
Ear, කන
Earth, පස, පොළොව
Eat, කනවා
Ebony, කළුවර
Either, වත්
Elephant, ඇතා, අලියා
Enquire, සෝදිසිකරනවා
Epidemics, වසංගතරෝග
Equal, සමාන
Every, සැම
Extent, ප්‍රමාණය

F

Face, මූණ
Fall, වැටෙනවා
Father, පියා, අප්පා
Fence, වැට
Fell, වැටුණ
Few, ටික
Feed, කවනවා
Fear, භය
February, පෙබරවාරි
Fist, මිට
Fibre, කෙන්ද
Fish, මාලුවා
Fire, ගිනි
Fire at, වෙඩිතිබනවා
Field, කුඹුර
Five, පහ
Fifty, පනහ
Fly, මැස්සා, පියාඹනවා
Flesh, මස්
Flower, මල
Flow, ගලනවා
Foot, අඩිය
Fool, මෝඩයා
Fox, නරියා, හිවලා
Frequently, නිතර
Friend, යහළුවා, මිතුරා
Fry, බදිනවා
Fruit, ගෙඩිය, ඵලය
Future, මතු
Furniture, ලීබඩු

G

Gamble, සූදුකෙළිනවා
Garden, වත්ත
Get, ලබාගන්නවා
Gem, මැණික
Give, දෙනවා
Girl, ගැනුලමයා
Go, යනවා
Goat, එළුවා
Goods, බඩු
Gold, රන්, රත්රන්

Great, ලොකු
Grass, තණ, තණකොළ
Grandfather, සීයා
Grief, කනගාටුව
Grow, වැවෙනවා

H.

Hand, අත
Have, තිබෙනවා
Harvest, මෝසම
He, ඔහු
Hearth, ලිප
Here, මෙහි, මෙතන
Hereafter, මින්පසු
His, ඔහුගේ
High, උස්
Honey, මීපැණි
Horn, අඟ
Home, ගෙදර
House, ගේ
Horse, අශ්වයා
How, කොහොමද
Hundred, සියය
Husband, පුරුෂයා
Hunter, වැද්දා, දඩයක්කාරයා

I.

I, මම
If, නම්
Infant, ළදරුවා
Intoxicated, මත්වෙලා
Iron, යකඩ
Is, තිබෙනවා, ඉන්නවා
It, ඒක

J.

Jack, කොස්
Jackal, හිවලා
June, ජූනි
July, ජූලි
Jungle, කැලෑව
Jump, පනිනවා

K.

Kandy, මහනුවර
Keeper, ප්‍රවේසම්කරන්නා
Key, යතුර
Kiss, සිඹිනවා
Kill, මරනවා
King, රජ්ජුරුවෝ

Knife, පිහියේ
Know, දන්නවා
Knee, දණ
Kuruni, ⅛ of a bushel

L.

Last, පසුගිය
Lad, කොල්ලා
Land, ඉඩම
Lately, මෑතදී
Lame, කොර
Lame man, කොරා
Letter, ලියුම
Let, ඉඩඅරිනවා
Learn, ඉගනගන්නවා
Lessons, පාඩම්
Lizard, හූණ
Leopard, දිවියා
Line, ඉර
Lion, සිංහයා
Little, පුංචි

M.

Mat, පැදුර
May, පුළුවනි, මැයිමාසේ
Mad man, පිස්සා
Man, මිනිහා
Make, සාදනවා
Marry, කසාද බඳිනවා
March, මාර්තු
Medical man, වෙදා
Measure, මනිනවා, මිම්ම
Me, මට
Mean, නීච
Met, සම්බවෙනවා
Milk, කිරි
Minute, මිනිත්තුව
Month, මාසේ
Mouth, කට
Moon, හඳ
Mountain, කන්ද
Mother, අම්මා, මව
Monkey, රිළවා
Money, කාසි
More, වඩා, තව
Moreover, තවද
Monday, සඳුදා
Moment, මොහොත
Much, බොහොම, පමණ
Must, ඕනෑ
My, මගේ

N.

Name, නම
Narrow, පටු
Nature, ස්වභාව
Narrowly, යන්තම්

Neck, බෙල්ල
New, අලුත්
New moon, අමාවක
Neither, වත්, නෑ
Near, ලඟ
Neighbour, අසල්වාසියා
Neighbourhood, අසල
Necessary, ඕනෑ
Nephew, බෑනා
Necklace, ඇටවැල
Net, දැල
Never, කවදාවත්නෑ
Next, ඊළඟ
Night, රාත්‍රිය
Niece, ලේලි
Nine, නවය
No, නෑ
Not, නෑ
November, නොවැම්බර්
Noble, උතුම්
Noise, ශබ්දය
Noon, මද්දහන, දවාල
North, උතුර
Now, දැන්
Nnmber, ගණන

O.

Obedient, කීකරු
Obtain, ලබාගන්නවා
October, ඔක්තෝබර්
Office, කන්තෝරුව
Old, නාකි, පරණ, මහලු
On, උඩ, පිට
Open, *v.* අරිනවා
Or, නොහොත්, වත්, හෝ
Our, අපේ
Over, වැඩිදුර
Ox, හරකා
Oyster, බෙල්ලා

P.

Pan, වලඳ
Paper, කඩදාසි
Patient, ලෙඩා
Parrot, ගිරවා
Paddy, වී
Pain වේදනාව
Pair, කුට්ටම
Pawn, උකස්කරනවා
Pardon, සමාව
Parent, මව්පිය
Peacock, මොනරා
Peace, සමාදානය
People, මිනිස්සු
Pepper, ගම්මිරිස්
Perish, නාස්තිවෙනවා
Perfect, සම්පූර්ණ
Pig, ඌරා
Pit, වළ

Piece, කෑල්ල
Place, ඉඩම
Plough, හානවා
Plumbago, මිණිරන්
Play, සෙල්ලම්කරනවා
Plaintiff, පැමිනිලිකාරයා
Plunder, කොල්ලකෑම
Pleasure, සතුට
Poor, දුප්පත්
Pour, වක්කරනවා
Post Office තැපල්කන්තෝරුව
Power, බලය
Prevail, පවතිනවා
Present, ඉදිරිපිට
Prevent, වලක්වනවා
Punish, අවවුකරනවා
Public, ප්‍රසිඩ

Q.

Quadruped, සිව්පාවා
Quality, ගතිය
Quantity, තරම
Quarrel, දබරය, දබරකරනවා
Quarter, කාලක්
Queen, බිසවුන්නාන්සේ
Question, ප්‍රශනය, ඇසීම
Quick, ඉක්මනින්
Quiet, නිශ්චල
Quite, හොඳටම

R.

Rat, මීයා
Raft, පහුර
Rafter, පරාලය
Rate, ගණන
Raw, අමු
Rain, වැස්ස, *v* වහිනවා
Remedy, පිළියම
Red, රතු
Red ant, දිමියා
Reap, ගොයම් කපනවා
Regularly, පිළිවෙළින්
Require, ඕනෑකරනවා
Report, රපෝර්තිය
Report, *v.* රපෝර්තිකරනවා
Ready, ලෑස්ති
Real, හරි
Rear, *v.* ඇතිකරනවා
Recollect, මතක්වෙනවා
Refuse, එපාකරනවා
Remain, නවතිනවා
Rent, බද්ද
Renter, රේන්දකාරයා
Repair, අලුත්වැඩියා කරනවා
Rest House, තානායම
Revenue, ආදායම
Rheumatism, ප්‍රමේහය

River, ගඟ
Ridge, නියර
Rice, හාල්, බත්
Rich, පොහොසත්
Right, හරි
Riot, කෝලාහලය
Road, පාර
Row, පදිනවා
Root මුල
Rob, කොල්ලකනවා
Rock, පර්වතය
Rogue, තක්කඩියා
Roof, වහල
Rope, ලනුව
Round, වටේට, වටකුරු
Run, දුවනවා
Rush in, වදිනවා
Rub, ගානවා, උලනවා
Ruin, නැතිකරනවා
Rubbish, රොඩු
Rust මලකඩ

S.

Sad, කනගාටු
Safe, ප්‍රවේසම්වූ
Salary, පඩි
Sale, විකිණීම
Salt, ලුණු
Sand, වැලි
Saturday, සෙනසුරාදා
Saw, කියත
Say, කියනවා
Scarce, දුර්ලභ
Scatter, විසුරුවනවා
School, සෝලය
Scissors, කතුර
Scrape, සූරනවා
Sea, මුහුද
Season, ඍතුව
Seat, අසනය
Second, දෙවෙනි
Secret, රහස
Security, ඇපය
See, දකිනවා
Seed, බිත්තර
Seize, අල්ලනවා
Seldom, කලාතුරකින්
Sell, විකුණනවා
Send, අරිනවා
Sensible, සිහිඇති
Separate, වෙනස්
Serpent, සර්පයා
Servant, වැඩකාරයා
Seven, හත
Several, කිප
Share holder, කොටස්කාරයා
Shape, හැඩය
Shares, කොටස්
She, ඈ
Sheep, බැටළුවා
Shine, බබලනවා
Ship, නැව
Shoe, සපත්තුව
Shore, වෙරල
Short, කොට, මිටි

Show, *v*, පෙන්වනවා
Shut, *v*, වහනවා
Sick, ලෙඩවූ
Side, පැත්ත
Sign, සලකුණ
Silent, *adj*, නිශ්ශබ්දවූ
Silver, රිදී
Sin, පව
Since, පටන්
Sink, කිඳනවා
Sir, මහත්මා
Sister, සහෝදරී
Sister-in-law නෑනා
Sit, *v*, වාඩිවෙනවා
Six, හය
Sixty, හැට
Size, තරම
Skin, හම
Skin, *v*, හමගහනවා
Sky, අකාශය
Slave, වාලා, දාසයා
Sleep, *v*, නිඳගන්නවා
Slowly, හෙමින්
Small, පුංචි, කුඩා
Small-pox, වසූරිය
Smoke, දුම
So, එසේ
Soap, සබං
Soft, මෘදු
Some, සමහර
Sometimes, සමහරවිට
Son, පුතා
Soon, ඉක්මනට
Sorrow, කනගාටුව
Sound, ශබ්දය
Sowing, වපුරන
South, දකුණ
Sowing extent, වපුරන ප්‍රමානය
Spit, *n*, කෙල
Spit, *v*, කෙල ගහනවා
Spoil, නරක්කරනවා
Spoon, හැන්ද
Spot, ස්ථානය
Spread, පැතිරෙනවා
Squirrel, ලේනා
Stand, හිටිනවා
Stamp, මුද්දර
Star, තරුව
Steal, *v*, හොරකම්කරනවා
Stealthily, හොරෙන්
Stick, කෝටුව
Stolen, සොරකම්කරපු
Stone, ගල
Stop, *v*. නවතිනවා
Straw, පිදුරු
Street, වීදිය
Strongly, තදේට
Such, අසවල්
Sudden, හදිස්සි
Sufficient, සෑහෙන
Sugar, සීනි
Summons, සිතාසිය
Sunset, ඉරබහිනවා
Sun, ඉර
Surely, සත්තකටම
Swallow, *v*. ගිලිනවා
Swear, දිව්රනවා
Swim, පිනනවා
Sweep, පිසදමනවා

T.

Tamil, දෙමළ
Tank, වැව
Take, ගන්නවා,
Table, මේසෙ
Tall, උස්
Tail, වල්ගය
Talk, දොඩනවා
Taste, රස
Tame, හීලෑ
Tavern, තැබෑරුම
Tax, අයබද්ද
Tauto-logy, පුනරුත්
Tears, කඳුළු
Tell, කියනවා
Temple, දේවාලේ, විහාරේ
Tear, *v.* ඉරනවා
Teach, උගන්වනවා
Thief, හොරා
Thread, නූල
This, මේ, මේක
That, අර
These, මේ, මේවා
Then, එවිට
There, එහි
Three, තුන
Thirty, තිහ
Third, තුන්වෙනි
Therefore, ඉත්නිසා
Thursday, බ්‍රහස්පතින්දු
Throw, *v.* විසිකරනවා
Theft, හොරකම
Thing, දෙය
Thirst, *n,* පිපාසය
Those, ඒවා
Though, නුමුත්
Tiger, දිවියා
Tiles, උළු
Timber, ලීදඬු
Time, කාලය
Tortoise, ඉබ්බා
Toddy, රා
Towards, දෙසට
Took, ගත්තා
Today, අද
Tommorrow, හෙට
Together, එක්ව
Top, මුදුන
Total, මුළුගණන
Town, නුවර
Tree, ගහ
Trample upou, පාගනවා
Trouble, වෙහෙස
True, සැබෑ
Trouth, සැබෑව
Tub, බාල්දිය
Twig, ඉත්ත
Two දෙක, දෙදෙන
Twelve, දොළහ

U.

Ugly, කැත
Umbrella, කුඩේ
Uncle, මාමා, බාප්පා
Under, යට

Undergo, දරනවා
Undertake, භාරගන්නවා
Unless, මිස, හැර
Until, තුරු, දක්වා
Up, උඩ
Upon, උඩ, පිට
Urgent, ඉක්මන්
Use, *n.* පාවිච්චිය
Use, *v.* පාවිච්චිකරනවා
Useful, ප්‍රයෝජනවත්
Useless, අප්‍රයෝජන

V.

Vain, නිෂ්ඵල
Various, නොයෙක්
Verb, ක්‍රියාවචන
Very, බොහෝම
Victory, ජය
Village, ගම
Visit, බලන්ටයාම
Voice, ශබ්දය, හඬ
Vomit, වමනය කරනවා
Vowel, පණ්කුර

W.

Wash, සෝදනවා
Washerman, රදවා
Way, මග
Walk, *v.* ඇවිදිනවා
Water, වතුර
Wave, රැළ
Wast-lands, හිස්ඉඩම්
Wages, කුලී
Wall, බිත්තිය
Want, ඕනෑ
Warrant, වරෙන්තුව
Watch, *v.* මුරකරනවා
Well, ළිද
We, අපි
Weave, වියනවා
Weaving, ගෙත්තම්
West, බස්නාහිර
Well, හොදයි
Weak, දුර්වල
Week, සතිය, සුමානය
Wealth, වස්තුව
Wedding, මංගල්‍ය
Wednesday, බදාදා
White, සුදු
Whisper, කොඳුරනවා
Who, කවුද
Whose, කාගේද
Whom, කාටද, කාවද
When, කවදාද
Why, මන්ද
Which, කෝකද
Where, කොතනද
What, මොකද
Wind, හුළඟ
Wife, ස්ත්‍රී, භාර්‍යාව
With, සමග

Wicked, නපුරු
Without, නැතුව
Wide, පලල්
Window, ජනේලය
Wild, වල්
Will, කැමැත්ත
Wing, අත්හැඩි
Wise, නුවණ ඇති
Witness, සාක්ෂිකාරයා
Woman, ගෑනි
Worm, පණුවා
Work, වැඩේ
Work, *v.* වැඩකරනවා
World, ලෝකය
Worth, වටිනා
Wrong, වැරදි
Written, ලියාපු

Y.

Yam, අල
Yard, යාරය
Year, අවුරුද්ද
Yearly, අවුරුදුපතා
Yellow, කහපාට
Yes, ඔව්
Yesterday, ඊයේ
Yet, තවම
You, උඹ, තමුසේ, තමුන්නාන්සේ
Youth, තරුණයා
Young, තරුණ, බාල
Young man, ඉලන්දාරියා
Young woman, ලමිස්සි
Younger brother, මලයා
Younger sister, නංගී